THEOLOGY OF MONEY

The Slow Collapse of the Anglo-Saxon Order

Jorge Majfud

Humanus

SAN DIEGO-ACAPULCO

Theology of Money. The Collapse of the Anglo-Saxon Order
© Jorge Majfud (English, 2025)
ISBN: 978-1-956760-44-6
Teología del dinero: El lento derrumbe del orden anglosajón
© Jorge Majfud 2023
© Humanus | March 2023
humanus.info
E-Mail: editor@humanus.info

Index

FEUDAL CAPITALISM

Theology of Money (2002)[1]

Once, a vassal was bound to his lord by an oath. A breach of the rules could mean a beating for the peasant. For the unfortunate, what mattered wasn't the stick but the King or Lord issuing the order. The Lord represented both protection and punishment. Yet, that unjust social relationship was still person-to-person: the peasant could see the Lord, and might even kill him with a stick just as sturdy as the one used on him.

The relationship that binds us to Money today is entirely abstract. In this, our society resembles the Middle Ages: we fear a symbolic, invisible entity, just as men feared God a thousand years ago. Stock values fluctuate without our involvement. Between those values and us lies a theology of money called "economics," which usually aims to rationally explain something that has no more rationality than symbolic power.

---

[1] Published in the journal *Bitácora* of the newspaper *La República* in Montevideo on November 6, 2002.

Our societies, like all others throughout history, are structured around power dynamics. As always, power is unevenly distributed, but in our time, it comes from Money. Thanks to money, we are all shareholders in the Power that rules the world, though our shares are infinitesimal. We know the sums accumulated in the world's major financial centers: they are many times greater than the combined efforts of dozens of third-world—and intermediate—countries. This simple fact means that Law and Freedom are overwhelmingly concentrated in certain financial capitals.

Let's consider this idea of freedom. In high school, we were taught that even a prisoner is a free being. This is rigorously true from an existential perspective, and a cynical assertion from an ideological one, especially when such truths were taught as free men were being imprisoned. Today, we live under a form of subtle, planetary dictatorship. Our governments tirelessly proclaim that this New Order is Inevitable. To question it is merely delaying its triumphant arrival. And, as far as I know, the Inevitable is not a product of freedom.

There is an immanent freedom in every human being, true; we are free the moment we hesitate at a crossroads. And there is another type of freedom: social freedom. This is not immanent but eventual. In our case, social freedom is doubly limited: first, because, in fact, the peripheral man is not free; second, because he has been made to believe he is. To say that the globalized man is socially free is like saying he is free as a bird. But a bird possesses bird-like freedom, that is, an "inhuman" freedom, since it cannot choose the direction or timing of its migration. A truly free man, on the other hand, should be able to do so.

Well; the choice of birds is determined by the power of nature. But at some point in history, we assumed that man had emancipated himself from this power, thanks to the irreverence of his spirit. And perhaps he has, to some extent. Then, what power has this incredible creature now succumbed to...?

Let's call it Money.

Let's see. The power of money is always symbolic: it comes from external recognition. All the power concentrated in banks originates from those who are harmed by that power; not from those who benefit from possessing it. Possession is an act of faith; non-possession is a condition of fidelity.

However, there are two values that are not merely symbolic: the value of violence (claimed as a monopoly by all governments) and the value of technology. In this new century, the power-value of technology will subdue the former and, despite its democratic possibility, will quickly be absorbed by the power-value of money. Yet, Money possesses a weakness hidden deep within its core: it is an abstract symbol that needs to be constantly fed with meaning. For this very reason, it hastens to dominate the power-value of technology. This new weapon will be used, in the coming century, for a ruthless struggle of interests: the caste of the productive against the financial caste, the Displaced against the Settled, the owners of Truth against those who suffer it.

Money is amoral, we know that. As we said, it is a symbolic, abstract power; it is worth what it is not and is all things at the same time. We believe we use it and subject it to our will, but it is It that subjects us: we can scarcely do without it, except through a dangerous act of heresy. Each day, we are less able to do without it.

To the ancient "basic needs," we have added an innumerable set of "social needs." We are born and develop in sophisticated societies that demand concentration. Like cattle, we are condemned to graze all day, to ruminate and to digest when we rest. A careless moment would mean falling out of the system. A social death, the true death of postmodern or posthuman man.

In our lagging world, the anguish is double: fulfilling social needs (now basic) occupies almost all our freedom. We want to be free, but freedom is expensive. So, we look to where money is abundant. Unlike other times, now we cannot usurp its place. We cannot invade them; therefore, the solution is to let them invade us. We copy. We want to resemble them: because they have triumphed in war and commerce, because they are rich and we are poor. It is also true: we want to stop being poor. But we will remain so as long as we think wealth is achieved by absorbing the cultural and moral values of the victor. Because integrating into the world is not the same as letting oneself be ingested. We too belong to the world, to the majority of the world, and though we may feel ashamed of our loincloths, we must remember that poverty is not proof of our moral vices. That is a religious idea of the Protestant world inherited by the North and sold to us in the South.

Throughout history, there have been great empires, dominant cultures; but never before have peripheral peoples (or the subjugated) stubbornly tried to mimic the victor, dismissing their own memory with alarming frivolity. On the contrary, in the past, it was the conquered peoples who infiltrated their own culture into the heart of the invaders. Today, we lack such dignity; the conquered peoples make themselves up to resemble the conqueror, forgetting and scorning the moral depth of economically impoverished civilizations, in exchange for mirrors and quick thinking. And yet, the rich world needs the poor world as much as these need them. Or more.

We are told that we live in a "globalized" world, but the only ones who have yet to realize its meaning are them, the ones responsible for globalization. As a practice, "globalization" is almost as old as Christianity. But now it stands on its own; it is a new ideology, with the historical peculiarity of having been preceded by its own realization. Its interpretation is also peculiar and always contradictory: to integrate means to absorb, to know means to ignore, cultural diversity means uniformity, to inform means to distort, wealth means money, and so on.

The borders remain the same for the poor, and have even closed tighter than before; however, they have been erased with a stroke of the pen to let Money pass through, carrying new promises of wealth to those poor countries that, one might wonder why, have seen their poverty increase. All of which leads us to say, without fear of being wrong, that in our globalized world, borders have been replaced by filters.

Culture and education no longer unite; they divide. Both have been subjected to the power of money and serve It to organize it into castes and accumulate it in invisible deposits. The new universities no longer care about wisdom or the pursuit of truth, but rather a single, monotonous objective: the creation of competent entities.

The North represents everything primitive in man: the overflowing need for power, accumulation, and consumption. All those spiritual values that emerged after the Mesolithic are beginning to be set aside. The repair is not near (only evangelicals see things as eternally imminent), because even the historical rebellion of youth has been indoctrinated by advertising and the success of others.

We agree that change is needed. But in what direction? Toward the North? One thing must be clear to us: there are changes that can only be generated by society as a whole. Therefore, the ideological precept summarized in the maxim, "If you don't like it, you're free to change the channel," is invalid. This phrase, so beloved by the profound philosophers of show business, is contradictory, not only with the much-touted idea of globalization but, above all, with the most primitive idea of society.

I, for one, am not against the North or against globalization. On the contrary, I would support it enthusiastically. That is, as long as Globalization means "dialogue" between cultures, between peoples, and between individuals; a true exchange of symbols and material goods, and not the simple imposition of languages, social and economic ideologies, or the imposition of monocultural customs that have led to the suppression of dozens of languages along with their knowledge of the sky and the earth, while also leading to the exploitation of natural resources that not only threaten the economically weaker communities but the entire planet.

But let's not be naive. Let's not forget that Money does not accept any other types of associations except associations of capital. Any other alliance, social or spiritual, will be condemned by Success. Remember: except for laughter and suffering, everything is a Universal Illusion: Success and Money do not exist without the value granted by those who are harmed by Success and Money.

20 YEARS LATER

The Dogma

In 1919, an event took place in the Michigan Supreme Court with ideological consequences that now span over a century, though its roots lie in 16th-century England, as we will explain in a forthcoming book—something to read with less urgency and anxiety—at least that's the superstition of every writer who wastes their life researching things that interest few and benefit even fewer.

A paradoxical protagonist and victim was Henry Ford, one of the many millionaires who admired Hitler and was decorated by him, with an aristocratic and racist view of societies. Seven years later, his decision to grant his workers one of the most long-demanded rights by unions in the West, the eight-hour day (8-8-8, eight hours for work, eight for rest, and eight for living), was based on the idea that workers should have the time and purchasing power to expand the businesses of those above. Like Hitler, Ford had also set out to produce a car for the people (Volkswagen) that could carry a man at the wheel, his wife by his side, and three children in the back.

By the second decade of the 20th century, and due to the success of the Ford T models that still roll through the streets of the old Portuguese city of Colonia del Sacramento in

Uruguay, Ford Company had accumulated an excess of capital, prompting its manager, Henry Ford, to decide to increase his workers' wages. To a large extent, this was a publicity strategy and, above all, Ford's suspicion that some shareholders were amassing profits to open their own company and compete with his (like the Dodges, who were already supplying mechanical parts to Ford itself), but in practice, it was going to benefit the company's workers.

As soon as they learned of Henry Ford's plans to let some of the profits trickle down to his workers, brothers John and Horace Dodge, who held ten percent of the company's shares, sued Ford Co., arguing that the accumulated capital belonged to the shareholders, not the workers, whose wages were already competitive in the market. Why more? The lawsuit was based on the accusation that the workers were stealing money that rightfully belonged to the investors.

In 1919, the Michigan Supreme Court ruled in favor of the Dodges, which not only allowed them to receive extra capital to start their own Dodge Automobile Company and flood the rest of the world with millions of friendly cars as proof of the benefits of capitalism, but, more importantly, it set a judicial, cultural, and ideological precedent. Since then, decisions by other courts and other mediums turned into written dogma the idea that capital and its profits belong to the shareholders, not the workers.

Explicitly, the state Supreme Court determined that company managers must administer their companies for the benefit of their shareholders, not for the charity of their workers. A philosophy that closely resembles that of the slave system, abolished half a century earlier but still alive and well in the rest of dominant culture, reproduced and practiced from media mogul William Hearst to each of the CEOs of the country's most powerful transnational corporations. It goes without saying that the same obvious truths were adopted and defended as life in the colonies of the Global South—and little has changed since then.

Political democracies, economic dictatorships

From France to Uruguay, not by coincidence, neoliberal governments have proposed pension reforms that add years to the retirement age (two in France; up to five in Uruguay). The narrative justifying the increase in retirement age is twofold: (1) people live longer and therefore must work longer; (2) if these "necessary and painful reforms" are not implemented, the system will become underfunded and the country will lose competitiveness in the world, as other countries have already applied these same measures, *necessary* for the financial class and *painful* for the productive classes. The same narrative, plus a third threat, has been repeated for decades in the United States: (3) Social Security (an invention of the "communist president" Franklin D. Roosevelt during the Great Depression) is unsustainable, which is why the retirement age must be raised and, as far as possible, privatized. It doesn't matter that it has always been self-sustaining. Social insurances are just that: insurances, not risky investments.

Privatization was first put into practice in peripheral countries. The destruction of Allende's socialist democracy, fifty years ago, and the imposition of Pinochet's dictatorship had the declared intention of preserving the freedom of capital and using this country as a laboratory for the neoliberal theories of Hayek and Friedman. The "Chilean Miracle" stood out for its social and economic crises, despite the tsunami of dollars from Washington and the large corporations. The semi-private pension model was brought to Uruguay in 1996 and took only twenty years to fail. The damned State had to come to the rescue of those harmed by the geniuses of investments.

The difficulty of a single country, whether France or Uruguay, resisting this acceleration of theft from the working classes is due to the fact that these neoliberal policies have a global reach. Countries are hostages to large capitals that migrate from one country to another in a matter of hours, terrorizing populations with the threat of another economic crisis and forcing their rulers, democratic or not, to kneel before these feudal lords. On the other hand, the world's largest financial institutions, such as the IMF and the World Bank, are allies of this mafia. The WB defines itself as a development bank, but its practice indicates the opposite: it serves the interests of capital, informing minute-by-minute which countries are planning to vote on a law to protect their workers or to control banking through regulations. This way, its partners and clients can protect their investments by transferring their millions from one sovereign country to another, more friendly, better positioned in the ranking of "business freedom," another of those old functional fictions.

Since the 1980s, worker productivity in the United States and globally has steadily increased, while wages have remained stagnant or lost purchasing power. It doesn't take a genius to figure out where this gap between productivity and wages has gone. But they want more.

Another tender explanation for legislating against the will of the people is the classic idea that it's not unions that govern but elected governments. Yet in France, 70 percent of the population is against the pension reform, and their "government elected by the people" refuses to listen. This deafness is typical and is justified by another *ideolexicon*: "the government must act responsibly, not demagogically." Again: responsibility toward harassing capital; demagogy for exercising democracy, giving people their right to decide.

All of this could be solved with a more direct democratic system, something many have written about for decades, especially with the advent of new digital tools. If the French could decide through regular referendums, France would not have experienced the massive protests and urban destruction of recent weeks. But ordinary citizens have no effective tool other than rebellion, sometimes violent. Obviously, this idea of direct democracy is dangerous because it is an idea in favor of real democracy.

As history shows, capitalism is, by nature, antidemocratic. It developed through the brutality and massacres in its colonies; it strengthened itself through slavery; it consolidated itself with the numerous military dictatorships in Asia, Africa, and Latin America. It has even recently felt quite comfortable with Chinese communism. When capitalism coexisted with liberal democracies, it was not because it was a democratic system but because it is a great manipulator, to the point of convincing half the world that democracy and capitalism are the same thing, since both are based on freedom. What it conveniently forgets to clarify is that democracy refers to the freedom of the people, while capitalism understands it as the freedom of capital—that is, the dictatorial elite that today not only owns most of the world's wealth but also controls the global financial system and has a near-monopoly over dominant media.

The French have a long tradition of social protests, and they can afford to rebel in the streets, as few will accuse them of being underdeveloped. Uruguayans, despite their long tradition of democratic institutions like education, health, and individual rights, are much more timid in their demands. Their oligarchy, like all others, also has a long tradition of stigmatizing advances in real democracy, accusing any popular demand of being communist (a recipe inoculated by the CIA in the 1950s that survives thirty years after the Cold War) while doing so in the name of democracy and freedom.

The (re)solution for France is not easy in an international context hijacked by the masters of capital, who demand and even convince their slaves to work more years for the same ration, and to do so willingly. For Uruguay, given its context and size, it is even more difficult. But in both cases, if resistance to economic dictates succeeds, they could become dangerous examples.

For these reasons, the only long-term solution is the union of a new wave of Non-Aligned Countries or those associated by common interests (cultural and economic), such as Latin America.

But of course, we all know that the century-old solution of imperial capitalism has been disunity, demobilization, and demoralization of colonies and their own workers. This ideological inoculation is so long-lasting that today, in former colonies, nationalist movements are on the rise. With one detail: they are not the anti-colonial nationalism of the 1960s in Africa, for example, but a servile and parasitic reflection of imperial nationalism in their own colonies.

The Chilean miracle

On March 21, 1975, University of Chicago professor and Nobel Prize-winning economist Milton Friedman visited General Augusto Pinochet in Santiago. He is accompanied by his colleague Arnold Harberger, a propagator of the idea of objective economic analysis and the "use of analytical tools applied to the real world," illustrated by his famous and abstract Harberger Triangle. In earlier times, as was the dogma of the era, Harberger had associated capitalism with democracy, but now, due to bad experiences with the real world, it is clear that only one of them truly matters.

Chile is an experiment that, regardless of the outcome, will be sold even in its countries of origin, the United States and Britain. The ideas are not new, but politicians need examples to cite, short phrases, and simple images. The grand theory is called *Trickle-down theory* (Teoría del derrame) and the image is illustrated with a bottle of Champagne filling the glasses at the top of the pyramid of glasses. The problem with the allegory is that it assumes that the glass of the glasses neither grows nor stretches indefinitely, unlike the capacity of those at the top to accumulate what never trickles down to those below. The image also does not consider a similar figure that does not exist in English and that no translator can resolve, but in Spanish it is called "La ley del gallinero" (The Law of the Chicken Coop). What trickles down is not wealth, but the shit from the chickens at the top.

This novel ideology already existed at the end of the 19th century. Amid the great recession of the 1990s and the expansion of U.S. imperialism over the sea, the representative from Nebraska and presidential candidate, William Jennings Bryan, at the Democratic convention on July 9, 1896, in Chicago, put it in no uncertain terms: "There are those who believe that, if we legislate to make the rich richer, their wealth will trickle down to those below. Our idea as Democrats is that, if we legislate to make the masses more prosperous, their prosperity will rise to all classes above them." Bryan accused the legislators of being advocates for the "businessmen," and according to the Chicago Tribune the next day, the attendees applauded his words massively and continuously "like never before... for 25 minutes." Bryan lost the elections to McKinley in 1896 and in 1900, the first two elections where million-dollar donations from major corporations decided the outcomes despite the worst economic crisis since the country's founding.

In 1964, the professor and ideologue Milton Friedman had visited one of the many Latin American dictatorships supported by Washington, Brazil, and had proposed the same plan of privatizations and dismantling of the state. On that occasion, the new ideological dogma of neoliberalism had not yet been consolidated in either the dictatorships or the democracies of Latin America, and Brasilia decided not to follow the suggestions of the renowned U.S. professor, but rather the opposite path of national industrialization championed by the Argentine economist Raúl Prebisch and, in some ways also, by Argentina's Peronism and Brazil's unwelcome leftist Getúlio Vargas. At the time, Latin American universities were not Marxist (as they were accused of being by the CIA and the Creole oligarchy) but Keynesian, much like Franklin Roosevelt himself. Keynesianism was the number one enemy of a new wave that had Friedman and Hayek as its two messiahs.

Now, despite the sudden "Chilean Miracle sustained by millions of dollars from Washington, fear and inflation reach triple digits, and Friedman recommends another magical solution: a policy of shock, meaning layoffs, fiscal austerity, cuts to social services, and privatizations without regard to consequences, with the natural exception of the military and the other repressive apparatuses of the dreaded state. This recipe would later be repeated in several Latin American countries as an experiment and, incidentally, as a source of historic profits for the corporations friendly with the government. Augusto Pinochet, praised for his rectitude, would funnel millions of dollars into his secret accounts in foreign banks while state-owned Chilean companies were auctioned off at prices well below their market value. A flawless deal, for some.

Friedman was not the only academic star to manipulate the dictator. Friedrich von Hayek also visited Pinochet's Chile several times and even recommended the new Chilean model to Margaret Thatcher. Like Friedman and like Harberger, Hayek decided to abandon the idea of democracy as a principle and turned it into what for many it always was: an excuse and a tool. "I would prefer a liberal dictatorship to a democracy that does not respect liberalism," he declared on April 12, 1981, to a journalist from El Mercurio, the newspaper of Agustín Edwards, the protagonist of the boycott against Allende and the CIA's favored player for decades to plant their editorials. Upon returning to the United States, Hayek declared: "I cannot say that during my visit to Chile I found anyone who said that individual freedoms under Pinochet were inferior to those under Allende." Hayek must have imagined that the anyone was all dead—or that none of them were present in the elegant salons he was invited to in

Santiago. Similarly, the influential U.S. ambassador to the UN, Jeane Kirkpatrick, a known advocate of military force to resolve philosophical and moral disputes, visited Chile in August 1981 and held it up as a model for the rest of the world. A few months after her departure, Chile would descend into another economic crisis, which the major newspapers in the North would report in small print.

None of the Chilean theorists, so well educated in Chicago, emerged out of nowhere with the coup d'état of '73. When in the 1950s the sustained growth of the left in Chile became evident, the sending of economics students from the Pontificia Universidad Católica de Chile to the University of Chicago began. Not just to any department but to study under the direct tutelage of Milton Friedman and Arnold Harberger, the ideologues of the reaction against the current initiated by the four-time U.S. president, Franklin D. Roosevelt, through which the superpower returned, for a few decades, to social policies and for which he was accused of being a socialist. In 1958, Jorge Alessandri had narrowly defeated Allende by a slim margin of votes, and in 1964 the CIA successfully financed Frei's electoral campaign against Allende with at least ten million dollars of the time. In 1970, the money wasn't as effective, and Allende ended up defeating Jorge Alessandri, prompting the Washington mafia to resort to the traditional Plan B for other poor countries: a coup d'état and military dictatorship to save the country from some fashionable threat to freedom.

Thanks to this dictatorship and others in Latin America, the Chicago Boys, the economists trained in the ideology of Friedman and Hayek, were given free rein to act in Chile and other countries. This group, its ideologues, and its apologists centered their praises on the idea that they are the ones who have promoted the "free market" and "individual freedoms," two noble ideas if it weren't for the fact that there is no free market under an absolutely unequal relationship between countries—quite the opposite. Much less are there individual freedoms, as these policies require multiple military dictatorships first and, later, banking dictatorships over countries ruined and indebted by the earlier dictatorships. The free market and individual freedoms, under these policies, mean the freedom of some markets to impose their conditions and interests over the rest, and the freedom of a few individuals to decide over the many.

Pinochet was not only not economically harassed by Nixon, as Allende had been, but, like so many other friendly dictatorships on the continent, he received all possible benefits (moral, ideological, military, and economic) from the superpower. In October 1973, in a single month, Nixon approved $24 million for Pinochet just to buy wheat, eight times Allende's budget for the same item over the past three years. By 1974, Chile received 48 percent of all food aid destined for Latin America. Just so the Great Propaganda of success wouldn't fail.

Despite everything, poverty and unemployment not only continued to grow in the so-called Chilean Miracle (a myth propagated and disseminated by the powerful ultra-conservative Heritage Foundation, founded by Paul Wey-rich, Edwin Feulner, and Joseph Coors) but also, in the 1980s, the country plunged into a painful economic crisis that occurred simultaneously in other less successful dicta-torships on the continent. Those who handed over the coun-try and its natural resources to transnational corporations through a bloody dictatorship were not called "sellouts" but "patriots saviors of freedom." The ideas indoctrinated as dogma, simply due to a strategic decision by U.S. agencies, were also not called "foreign ideas."

It was a perfect operation, or nearly perfect. Another classic case of reverse ideology. The neoliberal mafia always accused any university group, social activists, or critical intel-lectuals of practicing the ideas of the Italian Marxist theorist Antonio Gramsci. However, while the traditional left was Gramscian in its analysis of reality and its natural critical re-sistance to power, the international right was always Gram-scian in the application of power through colonized ideas.

Milton Friedman returned to Chile in 1981. After giving several triumphant conferences on his economic model ap-plied in that country, Chile plunged into a deep economic crisis. The social crisis had already begun with the financial strangulation of Salvador Allende's government and had deepened in the lowest sectors of society, even during "The Miracle." Following the guidelines of the Chicago Boys, Pi-nochet privatized education, healthcare, and pensions. GDP plummeted by 13 percent, and industrial production by 28 percent. Unemployment skyrocketed. Once again, Chile received tsunamis of economic and financial aid from the north. After denying it to Allende's government, the World Bank and the Inter-American Development Bank helped the friendly dictatorship with $3.1 billion. The economy recovered in 1981, but a year later, it fell into another crisis that spread to other military dictatorships in the region. In Uruguay, it was called the "collapse of the peg," when the dollar surged to ruin thousands of smaller businesses. As a solution, the IMF and armies of specialists proposed more of the same.

In Latin America (driven by an unpayable external debt, a legacy of excessive loans to friendly dictatorships with fluctuating interest rates), only between 1985 and 1992, more than two thousand industries and public companies were auctioned off with a predictable result of prosperity: the minimum wage collapsed, and the number of billionaires multiplied several times. In Bolivia, between 1995 and 1996, its government, aligned with the assault, sold its main companies to vultures at bargain prices. As if losing sovereignty and the income from those companies wasn't enough, the new and successful private businessmen, who do everything better for the country's progress, raised the prices of basic utilities, such as water, by up to 200 percent. In Argentina and other countries in the region, the story was strictly the same, and it ended in the massive crisis of 2002.

Upon their return from Professor Milton Friedman's first trip to Chile, students at the University of Chicago, members of the Spartacus group, organized a protest against his collaboration with Pinochet's dictatorship. Naturally, the students were accused of immaturity and Marxism. Professor Friedman defended his friendship with Pinochet with a colorful argument that provoked laughter echoing across the university campus: "If Allende had been allowed to remain in power, it is possible that, in addition to a terrible economic crisis, thousands of dissidents would have suffered unjust persecution, imprisonment, torture, and many would have been killed."

Fifty years later, in 2019, tsunamis of Chileans filled the streets demanding a new constitution to replace the neoliberal constitution approved by Pinochet in 1980. The neoliberal wall cracks. For months, Chileans were repressed with impunity and brutality by the same repressive forces created by Pinochet, a kind of legalized paramilitarism called Carabineros. Before Pinochet, the Chilean army was constitutionalist. After years of ideological cleansing, persecution, and assassination of dissident officers, it became something else.

In 2020, Pinochetist commandos like Revolutionary Capitalism or La Vanguardia organized violent actions against the tide of reformist protesters. One of the leaders of these far-right groups will be identified as Sebastián Izquierdo. One of his associates, Roberto Belmar Vergara, will confirm: "*If the approve wins, believe me, we'll swap batons for rifles.*"

Despite everything, after a year of violent repression, the Chilean people will force the first plebiscite since the dictatorship. On October 25, 2020, eighty percent of the votes across the country will demand a new constitution, and nearly the same percentage will confirm the need for a Constitutional Convention to draft it. Across the entire country, only the majority of Colchane (a town of 1,700 inhabitants in the north of the country) and the neighborhoods of Lo Barnechea and Las Condes in Santiago, where the elite-patriot class resides, voters who chose Yes in the previous 1989 plebiscite to maintain Pinochet's dictatorship, will vote in favor of keeping the constitution of their hero and benefactor.

The Assault of the Millionaires

The discourses about the capital that millionaires contribute in taxes and how much the poor and middle class receive from this forced generosity are an entire literary genre. In fact, this genre is chiefly cultivated by those at the bottom, as stated by the propaganda genius Edward Bernays: you must never say that what you want to sell is good but rather make others say it.

That the poor and workers (forgive the redundancy) defend the rich as benevolent donors is the direct result of such a publicity strategy and, as Bernays himself knew, it's not just about mass inoculation but also the exploitation of consumer weaknesses, such as the desire to stand out from their peers and, one day, even if it's a very distant day, to become part of that unattainable elite.

In reality, millionaires give nothing to society. They only return, through taxes, a minimal portion of what they have taken from it thanks to their position of power in business (which is practically the only way to join the one percent club).

This return is conveniently labeled "wealth redistribution" as if it were a donation or a theft that those at the bottom, the lazy workers, commit against the hardworking and intellectually gifted at the top. But the same word hides the truth. It is not a "distribution" of wealth produced by a small sector of society, but a "redistribution" of wealth produced by society as a whole, not only the existing one but all societies that preceded us and left Humanity a legacy of knowledge, discoveries, inventions, social struggles, and progress.

In other words, every economic system is a system of wealth redistribution, whether from the top down through taxes or from the bottom up through production and consumption.

But social myths are functional for power and, as such, are semantic masks, ideological mirrors tasked with reflecting reality but in reverse. Since it's actually millionaires who steal from workers every day and on a massive scale (taking not only wealth but political representation), the ideological narrative insists that it's the wicked who want to take from millionaires to give to the poor with "taxes that punish success." This is another deeply entrenched myth in society, a product of the same propaganda process by those with disproportionate social power, that is, those who dominate the economy and finance, who own major media outlets or are their subsidiaries through advertising payments, who are overrepresented in politics.

The same logic leads to not a few workers (especially in the United States and its colonies) repeating another myth: it's the rich who create jobs. It's the rich who create prosperity.

Another myth states that the rich are successful because they know how to compete. Many of them may be creative, but their creativity isn't invested in creating something new but in seizing what's already created. The praise for private projects like Elon Musk's Space X is presented as the paradigm of private innovation. The paradox is that his entire space project is built on nearly a century of successes and failures by government space agencies like NASA, the Soviet Union's space program, and, long before, the discoveries and progress of Hitler's Nazi government in Germany. Space X not only utilizes this entire accumulated knowledge without investing a single penny in it but even uses NASA's facilities and its funding, which is taxpayer money.

The rich do not compete; they destroy competition. The rich do not create wealth; they accumulate it. The rich do not create knowledge; they hijack it: the rich do not create ideas; they demonize them.

Small and medium-sized entrepreneurs compete every day to offer a service and, in doing so, earn profits that allow them to survive and, if possible, prosper. But megacorporations like Amazon or Walmart base their success not on competition but on the progressive destruction of that competition, which begins with the annihilation of small businesses through practices like disguised "dumping" (selling at a loss). It then continues with the annihilation of other giants, as happened in the United States with various chains like Sears or Radio Shack. One could argue that Amazon's service is effective, but anyone at any point in history with a greater accumulation of capital will be effective because every new innovation will be at their disposal.

Now they are praised as those who "created the world we live in." What did Jeff Bezos invent? What did Bill Gates invent? What did Steve Jobs invent? What did Mark Zuckerberg invent? Historically speaking, nothing, apart from some makeovers on centuries of accumulated progress. Everything was invented before or after by others who did not become millionaires nor suffered from that terrible psychosocial pathology. From the algorithms invented by the Persian mathematician Al-Khwarizmi (or Algorithmi) in the 9th century to computers, the internet, software, email, social media, and all kinds of tools that, for better or worse, make our world possible, all or almost all were created by salaried inventors and researchers, and nearly everything was funded by some government. In most cases, capitalism didn't even exist as a historical stage, and when it did, its geniuses were not capitalists, with one or two dubious exceptions.

Let us not be confused by media propaganda or the cultural industry. The goal of every big business, every large corporation, is neither to contribute an invention to Humanity nor to benefit anyone other than its owners through the hijacking and accumulation of wealth, the product of a long history of technological and social progress, the result of the vast effort of the rest of society with its public and private institutions. Thinking otherwise is like insisting that the work of the fisherman who casts his nets into the sea is to reproduce fish. Every mega-corporation is just that: a gigantic fishing net. Everything else is nonsense, and not the best kind.

The millionaires justify themselves solely through their economic power, the propaganda that emanates from this power, and the political power they hijack to benefit their own businesses. This propaganda is so effective that it can falsify reality until a hardworking choripán vendor with two assistants identifies with one of these postmodern heroes (now deified as entrepreneurs) and directs his frustration and political rage against his class peers, who are only distinguished from him because they are employees, not bosses. But all three are workers; neither an entrepreneur nor Jeff Bezos nor Mauricio Macri.

A millionaire may be a good person, but their historic and social role is the legalized theft from the rest of society. A sexy theft, it must be said, because a large part of the people wants to be millionaires, as in fairy tales. But, as in fairy tales, only one poor Cinderella can marry the prince; not two, and certainly not a million. In the one percent club, there is no room for more, only for less.

The Latin Mafia and Elections in the United States

In December 1980, months after the assassination of Monsignor Oscar Romero and for the same reasons, four American nuns were ambushed on a road in El Salvador. After raping them, they were killed, buried in a pit, and the van they were traveling in was burned.

For years, the U.S. government tried to blame leftist guerrillas for the incident, where peasants fleeing the genocidal brutality of the Junta military government in El Salvador had sought refuge. But the families of the nuns were not convinced by the arguments coming from the White House and repeated in the mainstream media. After the Jesuit massacre in 1989 by the paramilitary group Atlácatl, another creation of the School of the Americas and responsible for multiple massacres, such as the one in El Mozote in 1981, cracks began to appear in the narrative, and the soldiers involved in the murder of the four nuns started to talk.

The American nuns and the Spanish Jesuits were human beings with names and last names, that is, people with rights. The 75 thousand Salvadorans massacred in just 12 years, the overwhelming majority by the military and paramilitary forces of the regime supported by Washington, were never enough to force any political change or the peace negotiations that followed in the 1990s.

Thousands of survivors of another genocide deemed unimportant managed to escape the massacres, the economic chaos, and the social terror that continued in what was conveniently called a "Civil War." The wives, children, and siblings of the massacred (in some cases, the army would grab children by their feet and smash them against rocks to save bullets), some of whom I know, like the poet Carlos Ernesto García, had to emigrate. Most came to the United States, simply because of job opportunities.

As in the rest of the dictatorships since the 19th century, that of the Revolutionary Junta, that of Napoleón Duarte, and that of the Salvadoran oligarchy was protected and funded by Washington and by private sectors. The same story happened in the Panama of the CIA's favorite drug trafficker, Manuel Noriega, in the Honduras of Battalion 3-16 (another paramilitary group trained by the CIA) and in the Guatemala of genocidal Ríos Montt, who not only received moral, military, and economic support from the government of Ronald Reagan but also from Protestant churches like that of the powerful televangelist Pat Robertson, the same man who supported dictatorships in Africa and who proposed in 2005 the assassination of Hugo Chávez as "the most economical way" to solve "the problem" of another democratically elected but disobedient president.

Once the *nobodies* fled the chaos of Central America and crossed the southern border of the United States, they were greeted with bullets by various paramilitary groups, like the CMA (*Civilian Materiel Assistance*, created by the CIA in 1984 to operate in Central America and with ties to the KKK in Alabama), and other mercenaries who in the 1980s had trained the terrorist group known as the Contras in Nicaragua. Once back in their country, they repeated the familiar rhetoric of "this is a country of laws, and we have the right to protect our borders from invaders."

While the victims of the barbarity imposed and funded in the former banana republics were being criminalized, the generals responsible for the massacres in those same countries, as tradition dictates, flew to Florida, where they began a new life, not coincidentally, full of business success. This was the case with the two generals responsible for the massacre of the four American nuns in 1980, Carlos Vides Casanova and José Guillermo García. In Miami, they put on suits and ties and started businesses with help from "the community." No one who saw them in meetings or walking the streets of Miami (except for a doctor and a professor who recognized them decades later) suspected that these respectable-looking men were, in fact, genocidal killers.

Similarly, very few could have guessed that terrorists like the Cubans Luis Posada Carriles, Orlando Bosh, and many others (in *The Wild Frontier* I detail several cases) classified as "terrorists" by the FBI itself were sunbathing on the beaches of Miami and meeting with the most "successful businessmen" in the country. All "freedom fighters" planning bombings (like the assassination of Orlando Letelier and his secretary with a car bomb steps away from the White House, or the bombing of Cubana Flight 455 that killed 73 people) or simply to harass or eliminate troublesome people using more conventional methods.

The list of mafia and terrorist organizations based in Miami is too extensive to include in an article, but suffice it to say that, with exceptions, it is consistent with their level of impunity, some due to their ties to the CIA and others due to their political connections. The Center for Justice and Accountability, based in California, records over a thousand foreign criminals, VIP class, living in the United States. Now, you don't need to be a genius to guess which candidates these "successful businessmen," responsible for various genocides, support.

In the most recent electoral campaign in the United States, the traditional press, television, and social media bombard us with political propaganda that is a copy of all previous campaigns. One of them is that of the powerful Florida senator, Marco Rubio (in Congress for 22 years), with the simplicity typical of McDonald 's' menu that the far-right loves so much. In all of them, the senator appears with images of poor immigrants crossing the border as if they were about to invade the still world-leading power. In other speeches, these men are accused of having a disproportionate sexual appetite, that is, the same accusation borne from the pornographic imagination that 19th-century slaveholders had about a possible liberation of slaves and the rape of little blond girls.

In one of those ads, Senator Rubio repeats a cliché I have already responded to before (UNESCO Courier, 2019):

"They accuse us of racism for defending our laws (and) for defending our borders" (October 2022). An old masterpiece of hypocrisy that, to resolve the contradiction between two terms, eliminates one. They eliminate history (in Florida, Governor DeSantis managed to ban its revision) and simplify it to a strategic degree, which is the best way to win elections.

This is how we arrive at the criminal hypocrisy of the powerful "Latino" establishment, especially in Florida, where the victims of barbarity designed in their countries (who, moreover, do not vote) are criminalized, while the genocidaires from those same countries enjoy legality and the old mafia network, and naturally, contribute money to the political campaigns of those who will benefit and protect them.

All in the name of freedom, the fight against communism, against heretics, and the alien invasion.

Capitalist patriotism

"On that national holiday, all the kids were herded into a courtyard and made to pledge allegiance to the flag. *'Do you swear to defend this immaculate symbol with your blood, regardless of what reasons you might have not to do so?'* To which the kids would shout back very loudly, *'Yes, with this blood,* I swear!' From then until death, the inhabitants of Calataid would proudly wear the scar of the Pledge to the Flag, which was not only essential for any public procedure, such as joining the honorable Pork and Chicken Feeders Guild to collect the traditional bribes, but it also served to practice an old custom that involved measuring it whenever two old friends met (…) '*When they pushed me with the other kids into the schoolyard to swear to that piece of cloth, I shouted very loudly* I do not swear! *But my* No *was lost among the obedient sworn yes's of my classmates.*'".

This moment from the cubist novel *La ciudad de la luna* (2009) is a fictional testimony of my experience as a first-year high school student during the military dictatorship in Uruguay. While the principal recited the patriotic phrases that made the parents cry, I remembered my grandfather, tortured by Captain Nino Gavazzo, later a prisoner accused of feeding some fleeing Tupamaros whom he didn't even know. I remembered my uncle, also tortured, and I remembered his young wife shooting herself in the chest. I was five years old, but I never forgot. I remembered the conversations in a farm in Colonia, where two men, facing the kitchen lamp, mentioned that the bodies appearing in the Río de la Plata were not fishermen but had been thrown from Argentine planes, more than ten years before one of the pilots confessed it in 1992.

When I asked the teacher of "Moral and Civic Education" what the laurel branch on the national shield meant, he hit my hand for pointing at the sacred symbol with a finger. The history teacher, a proud descendant of an English captain and tired of my questions, told me in front of the whole class that no relative of mine would ever have a street named after them. I didn't understand why that was important then, and I still don't now. Shortly after, I asked the literature teacher, a very kind woman, why Juan Carlos Onetti wasn't even mentioned, and her response was: "because the country gave him everything—education, work, family—and he went to another country to criticize his own."

Years later, when the budding democracy released the political prisoners from Libertad, one of them visited my grandfather's farm and told him that, together with a relative, they had opened a small restaurant and invited one of their comrades who was a singer. But one day, they asked him to include some songs that weren't protest songs. The musician took offense, and the friendship ended there. "He should understand that you can't keep your business running only with clients who think like us," my grandfather commented.

The revolutionary singer's attitude toward the context has something in common with the dialectical tactics of the *influencers* of capitalism. A popular Iranian YouTuber who emigrated to the United States and defines himself as "someone who loves this Great Country" once interviewed an American professor who identifies as a Marxist. After displaying a show of historical ignorance, he could barely muster the classic jab: "Why don't you go live in Russia?" Russia isn't even socialist, which makes the invitation to live in Cuba even more classic. The inquisitors don't bother to consider that Cuba is a consequence of U.S. imperialism and, even less, that it is in countries like Cuba where capitalism exerts its miraculous powers most strongly.

The tactic of questioning a person's private life as an argument against their ideas is mediocre and cowardly. Like questioning a socialist for sending their daughter to a private school because they want to and can afford a bilingual education. Like questioning a poor capitalist (or rather, someone who believes in capitalism) for sending their child to a public school. Or questioning someone because they live in one neighborhood and not another. Each individual lives in specific circumstances in a specific world; in any case, one dominated by capitalism.

Especially if they're a wage earner. When the neoliberal crisis hit Latin America at the beginning of the century (as a logical consequence of the forced indebtedness of the 70s, which later led to the IMF's prescriptions and the Washington Consensus in the 90s), many of those who had a white refrigerator inside and out emigrated to Europe or the United States as a way to survive and later, in some cases, for professional reasons. Some imposed ideological changes on themselves to avoid the discomfort of the false contradiction: if you live in a capitalist country, you must be capitalist. If you live in a socialist country, you must be… well, opinions vary.

Currently, the logical consequence of the growing social inequalities of neoliberalism and the loss of extractive power by imperial powers (euphemistically called *developed*), first over their colonies, then over their friendly dictatorships, and finally over indebted democracies in development, has given way to a more visceral fascism. This nationalist wave (not to be confused with imperialist nationalism with anti-colonialist nationalism) was born in "developed countries" and then, like everything else, was copied in their ex-colonies with an inferiority complex.

The advantage of fascism is not only its intellectual simplicity, illustrated by its tribal symbolism of flags, shields, chants, and clichés, but also its visceral and militaristic patriotism. The hatred of all kinds of others in the name of love for the country where they were born or the sudden, love-at-first-sight for the country they adopted.

Patriotism is not the love of a country but the reflection of self-love in foreign symbols. Love and hate for a country are two impossible fictions, but very useful ones. Sometimes it works to reclaim the rights of oppressed peoples. Sometimes, for the opposite. Generally, it is one of the collective passions easiest to manipulate by those at the top, the ones who couldn't care less about the homeland, the flag, or the lives of those who swear to die for them.

Psychopatriotism

Thanks to a 1994 law (*Holocaust Education Bill*), public schools in Florida have a subject called "Holocaust," through which students study the racist atrocities committed in Europe against the Jewish people. In 2020, Governor Ron

DeSantis enacted another law requiring all elementary and secondary schools to certify that they are teaching the new generations about the Holocaust. At the time, African-American senators ensured that the program also includes mention of the Ocoee Massacre, where 30 Black people were killed in 1920, which, to understand endemic racism and social injustices, is akin to explaining the human body through its shadow.

By law, since 2022, discussing the racist history of the United States is also prohibited in those same Florida high schools. The reason, according to Governor Ron DeSantis, is that "no one should be instructed to feel as if they are not equal or ashamed of their race. In Florida, we will not allow the agenda of the far left to take over our schools and workplaces. There is no place for indoctrination or discrimination in Florida."

If it's not talked about, it doesn't exist. On this side of the Atlantic, racism doesn't exist and never did.

The same enslavers who defined millions of slaves (the foundation of the country's prosperity) as "private property" based on their skin color called that system the "blessing of slavery," which they wanted to "expand worldwide" to "fight for freedom," while calling their system of government "democracy" (Brown, 1858).

The same ones who robbed and exterminated indigenous peoples far more democratic and civilized than the new nation of the gold rush before the gold rush called it "self-defense" against "unprovoked attacks" by savages (Jackson, 1833; Wayne, 1972).

The same ones who invented Texas' independence to re-instate slavery and then waged war against Mexico to seize half its territory, the same ones who killed and raped women in front of children and husbands, did so under the divine design of God's "Manifest Destiny" (Scott, 1846).

The same ones who practiced the sport of killing Black people in the Philippines did so to fulfill "the white man's burden" of civilizing the world (Kipling, 1899).

The same ones who invaded, corrupted, and plagued Latin America with banana republics, destroyed democracies, and planted dozens upon dozens of bloody dictatorships did so to fight for freedom and democracy (Beveridge, 1900; Washington Post, 1920; CIA, XXX).

The same ones who showered Asia with atomic bombs, millions of more benign bombs without a year's truce, chemical agents on millions of humans, and left thousands dead wherever they went called this extreme exercise of racism a "heroic victory," even when they were humiliating defeats (Johnson, 1964; Bush, 2003).

But none of this can be spoken of because it might offend someone with white skin who identifies with all those champions of freedom, democracy, and divine justice.

As a popular song once said to recruit volunteers for the invented war against Mexico:

Justice is the motto of our country

the one that is always right (Pratt 1847).

Not by chance, every time those groups of fanatics felt their privileges threatened by the never-accepted equality, they invented self-victimization theories, like the theory of "white extinction," articulated in the 19th century to justify colonialism and the oppression of non-Caucasian peoples (Pearson, 1893) and now reborn as a novelty like the "Replacement Theory," which criminalizes immigrants from non-European countries as "dangerous invaders" (Camus, 2010).

It is no coincidence that Adolf Hitler drew inspiration from the then-institutionalized racism of the extreme right in the United States, which indoctrinated millions to feel superior due to their skin color and millions more to accept their inferiority for the same reason (Grant, 1916).

It is no coincidence that Hitler decorated the great businessmen of the United States and prohibited the teaching of "leftist things" in public education. Before persecuting and killing Jews, in 1933 he shut down the renowned Bauhaus school for being full of "anti-Germans" and a "haven for leftists" who wanted to question and change history.

In Florida and across the country, education systems should begin with a subject called "Patriotic Hypocrisy" to develop, even slightly, the intellectual capacity to confront historical reality without sugarcoating and without the fantasies of Hollywood, Disney World, and the Ku Klux Klan.

We are not responsible for the crimes of our ancestors, but we are responsible for adopting them as our own when we deny or justify them. We are responsible for the crimes and injustices committed today thanks to the denial of reality that, not without fanaticism, we call patriotism. A criminal and racist denialism, as it once again denies justice and the basic right to truth for victims in order not to disturb the sensibilities of others, the dominant group for over two centuries, which insists on the strategy of self-complacency and self-victimization as a way to soothe their frustrations and foundational hatred. It is even worse when that right to truth has been severed by laws and a culture full of taboos, all in the name of a democracy that they find bothersome and use, just as the demagogues of ancient Athens used it to demonize and then execute Socrates for questioning too much. All legally, of course, until the laws are written by others.

What greater indoctrination than denialism or the prohibition of revisiting history? What greater indoctrination than imposing complicit silence or a "patriotic history" in schools, laden with myths created *post factum* and without documentary support?

Immigrants: the good slave and the rebellious slave

In the Middle Ages and during the European Renaissance, the title of hidalgo could have meant "son of something" or "loyal to his master." Though its etymology is debated, what's clear is that it referred to an aspiring noble, a second-tier aristocrat. A noble did noble things by inheritance, while the common folk were vulgar, and the villagers were villains by nature. They were the sons of nobody. They were the faceless pawns of chess, without crowns, without hats, without horses, and without towers to take refuge in. They were the first to go die in the wars of the nobles, the first to defend the king and queen, though they never climbed the castle and certainly never entered the palace. In groups of a thousand, they formed militias. They were numbers. Like in modern wars, they went to kill and be killed, with fanaticism, defending a noble cause, in both senses of the word. God, country, liberty. Noble causes that concealed the interests of the nobles.

Little or nothing has changed since then. The American soldiers who return from the wars of their nobles disembark at Atlanta's airport and are applauded by the vassals who will later abandon them to the madness of their memories. Memories, and even forgetfulness, will haunt them like the devil. Many will end up in beggary, drugs, or suicide. When they no longer matter, they will be honored in nameless graves or have flowers laid on a fallen pawn, as abstract as in chess, called the Tomb of the Unknown Soldier. Especially if there are television cameras nearby.

Not to mention the figures, a thousand times larger, of the civilians killed on the other side, who aren't even clear numbers but estimates. Approximations that never reach the outrage of the major media or the comfortable conscience of

First World citizens, because the suppressed belong to inferior races, subhuman categories that want to attack us or threaten to take away our way of life by ceasing to be slaves. The attacks of the powerful nobles are so preemptive that they often eliminate fifty children in a single bombing without provoking speeches or outraged marches led by world leaders. Not even a timid January 6th in favor of peace and justice for others.

Medieval pawns and vassals had no faces or surnames because they had nothing to leave to their children as inheritance. They barely had a name and the reference of where they were born or what they did for a living, when working was a sign of shame and, as now, a sign of necessity. To say that someone cannot afford a prolonged rest is to call them a worker. Being the child of a working-class family is a euphemism for being poor. It's not so grave because, like inferior races, the poor have no feelings.

"The poor also feel their sorrows," says a servant in *The House of Bernarda Alba*, and Bernarda, the poor aristocrat, responds: "But they forget them in front of a plate of chickpeas."

The pain of those who are far from power doesn't matter, just as fifty children suppressed by a bomb in a distant country don't matter. Just as fifty children caged in an immigration facility don't matter. Just as undocumented migrants, poor and dark-skinned, don't matter, because they too are criminals who have violated Our laws by working for us as slaves and stealing a wage no slave deserves.

In antiquity, debt slaves were known as "addicts." They were those who *said*, who spoke on behalf of their masters. They were bound to servitude. Centuries later, when the invention of hereditary slavery based on skin color was outlawed in the 19th century, slavery once again became a matter of addicts. Now they are the poor bound to servitude by the necessity of their poverty, almost always hereditary, like the European poor who once sold themselves for five or ten years as slaves in North America.

But today's *indentured laborers* are not just immigrants who must sell themselves at the low price of necessity; they are also those who, without hunger and without a sick mother on the other side of the border, decide to sell their word in exchange for physical and moral comfort. Like slaves in ancient Rome, they are "addicts," not to a substance but to the values, morals, and ideas of their masters—the millionaires to whom we must thank for peace, order, and progress, just as in the 19th century enslaved Black people were expected to thank their enslavers for the shade of the trees, the rain, and the gruel they ate twice a day. As in the 19th century, the enslavers expanded with a rifle in one hand, the discourse of the struggle for freedom in the other, and their addicts behind them.

As Peruvian González Prada and American Malcolm X once denounced, these addicts ("the good Indian," "the good Black person") are the worst enemies of justice and the liberation of their own brothers. Language, which preserves an infinite hidden memory, also knows that the word lackey was the name of the sycophantic squires—greedy mercenaries who walked behind their masters like remora fish attached to sharks.

But there are also those who have not sold their freedom at the price of necessity and resist inoculating themselves with the myth of "The Land of the Free" to which "they came voluntarily" and can leave, also "voluntarily," paving the way for the remoras and the addicts. They are the undocumented immigrants who occupy the lowest ranks of the richest societies. Those who must sell their bodies but do not sell their consciences.

Often I have been asked if I am not afraid to write against imperial mafias from the belly of the beast, as José Martí once said. True, it's not easy, and I would gain much more by flattering power and adjusting my ideas to my personal interests. But there are things that not even all the billions of modern nobles can buy. Now, if we're talking about courage, the first prize goes to the undocumented immigrants. Especially immigrants like Ilka Oliva-Corado. Domestic worker, talented painter and writer, brave as a paper boat in a storm, woman, Guatemalan, proudly Black, and unbound in her speech. A worthy representative of the most suffering immigrants in the United States, expelled from their countries of origin, despised, exploited, and dehumanized by the societies that use them and by the societies that expel them only to later receive their remittances.

Is Fascism the Future of Humanity?

On October 29th, the hundredth anniversary of the March on Rome was commemorated, the assault that legally installed Benito Mussolini in power in Italy. On the same day, it was also the anniversary of the founding of Spain's Falangist Party, established by dictator Primo de Rivera in 1933 to begin the destruction of the Second Republic, a rare democratic experience that universalized voting and created thousands of public schools during its brief existence.

On October 29th of this year, a Nazi rock concert (also known as RAC, *Rock Against Communism*) titled "The Empire Strikes Back" took place in Mexico City, gathering 300 attendees convinced of their superior race. Tribal instincts reveled in promises to fight the inferior beings who deny them freedom.

The attendees were roused by the fascist band from Madrid, "Batallón de Castigo," (Punishment Battalion) formed in the 90s within a prison. Its members were not convicted for political reasons but for robbery and murder. All part of a powerful religion that venerates its own guts. Their shirts proudly displayed slogans like "For My Clan" (Clan as tribe and Klan, with a K, referencing the Ku Klux Klan). Precisely, the idea and obsession with the replacement and annihilation of "the beautiful race" had already been articulated in books published in the Anglo-Saxon empires in the late 19th century, all matured in the long experience of slavery and the frustrations of defeat in the Civil War, long before Hitler drew inspiration from these "patriots who love freedom." The digital universe gave fascists and neo-Nazis the protection of anonymity, which, over years of practice, honed their hatred and a few basic ideas, such as the "fight against communism" and "against gender ideology." Gradually, this catharsis led to the revival and reinforcement of an ideology that had spread a century earlier with the novelty of radio. From a frustrating stagnation, they transitioned to a gradual emergence from the closet, mainly through extreme-right political options without the Nazi paraphernalia.

After the Soviet Union defeated Hitler (with help from its ally, Washington), conservatives in the United States banned the entry of communists into the country. The American Communist Party was filled with Black members, and the FBI persecuted homosexuals for being potential communists. In 1954, they banned the party. They didn't mind hiring a thousand German Nazis for NASA and allowing another nine thousand "refugees" to enter. Even today, immigration and naturalization processes ask applicants if they have ever belonged to a communist party (Donald Trump's in-laws skipped that question) but ask nothing about membership in fascist or neo-Nazi groups.

In Mexico, Nazis did not achieve the overwhelming success they had in the United States before the war. Their membership barely reached 150 enthusiasts. The relationship between Lázaro Cárdenas' government and Hitler was purely strategic (replacing the United States as a client for a few years made possible the nationalization of Mexican oil). More intense and ideological was Hitler's relationship with Washington and, above all, with the great businessmen of that country.

But the fascists and neo-Nazis penetrating Latin America today are better organized and more dangerous, even more dangerous than the Nazis who escaped to South America or those sent by the CIA to "fight communism," supporting dictatorships that protected transnational corporate interests.

Now, between November 28th and 29th, dozens of far-right international politicians will gather in Mexico City at an event organized by the Viva México Movement and the Conservative Political Action Conference (CPAC, Conservative Political Action Conference) in a fascist international assembly. After decades, CPAC has decided to leave the United States and hold propaganda events in Brazil and Mexico.

Attending this event will be, among others, the Chilean son of a Nazi, staunch Pinochetist, and businessman José Antonio Kast; Argentina's Boris Johnson, Javier Milei; Brazilian President Bolsonaro's son Eduardo Bolsonaro; Donald Trump's strategist and instigator of the Capitol assault, Steve Bannon; and the grandson of dictator Rafael Trujillo and American businessman, Ramfis Domínguez-Trujillo; the daughter of Guatemalan genocidal leader Efraín Ríos Montt and congresswoman from her country, Zuri Ríos; and a few dozen other distinguished speakers. All Caucasian and with a preference for blue eyes, with the sole exception of Indo-

American Shiva Ayyadurai, who presents himself as "The inventor of email," despite the fact that email had already been developed while he was a child in India. But well, we know that for these people, reality doesn't matter, only what they believe and claim to be true.

The first speaker will be the ultra-conservative Catholic Lech Walesa, who claims that "sexual minorities oppress heterosexuals." In many of them, from Trump to Milei, body language is more important than their ideas. Their furious speeches resemble those of Hitler and Mussolini. Then and now, they express the frustration of a class that already knows it is no longer an empire or that it no longer rules over the masses, but doesn't know who to blame except those below who can't even defend themselves with a vote, as is the case with immigrants.

Despite the much-touted *patriotism*, in Latin America, right-wing ideologies have been imported and imposed from above and from abroad. The cultures of native peoples have always been more aligned with what in the West has been called "the left." One of the CPAC attendees, the Mexican and Texas congresswoman Mayra Flores, insists that "Mexicans are conservative." She refers to the Anglo-Saxon dogma of "private enterprise" and corporations. The indigenous communities of Mexico, like those throughout the Americas, had to endure dispossession through the imposition of privatization of their lands and lives, from Porfirio Díaz's Mexico to the neoliberal wave a century later. This age-old tradition, demonized as socialist, doesn't count as conservative.

"We will be here, defending America's freedom," says a promotional phrase for the event. Whose freedom? The freedom of the elites, supported by a portion of those below thanks to political combos that include a bit of religion and "traditional values," such as family, machismo, and hatred for those even further below. It is the same fight for freedom as the 19th-century slaveholders who claimed they were expanding slavery to "fight for civilization" and "freedom." One of the presentations (titled "How to Save Religious Freedom?") is a right-wing classic. It assumes that religious freedom is exercised when their sacred religion is imposed on a government and the evil of secularism is fought. Not without irony, secularism, the separation of church and state, was invented to protect religious freedoms, including the right to have no religion.

The American Conservative Union (ACU) and CPAC emerged and took control of the Republican Party in the 60s and 70s, as a reaction to defeats against Martin Luther King's Civil Rights Movement and others. This "Empire Strikes Back" movement is also a reaction, not only to the wave of defeats in Latin America but, above all, to the awareness that this order is unsustainable and sooner or later, a generation will arise that will threaten the privileges of those at the top.

If we could stand in 1922 and ask ourselves *"Is fascism the future?"* we wouldn't know how to answer. By 1940, we would have answered *yes* and then*no* five years later.

Once fascism manages to extend its power as far as its desires reach, it will leave behind a trail of destruction and death. Then they will flee like rats, once again, back into anonymity and self-victimization.

Social networks are of the right

In *Critique of Pure Passion* (1998) and later in articles published in newspapers, I wrote, with enthusiasm, various theories about the marvelous world of past centuries that I had lived in Africa and about the equally fascinating world to come. Youth, divine treasure…

In Mozambique, at the Pemba Naval Shipyard, I discovered and collaborated (as a young architect from America, whom hundreds of kind workers mistakenly called "maestro") in the construction of large British and Portuguese ships from the 19th century. Through the shipyard (the marvelous umbila trees were raw material) and to support a technical school program in the most populated cities, I often traveled for long hours to the "mato" (Ibo, Quisanga, Montepuez, Mueda, Macimboa, Matemo), to the tribes far removed from the privilege of the white man, of which I was a part. At the shipyard, I also had contact with the racist Boers of South Africa, with the British-American anti-apartheid writer Joseph Hanlon, and with the son of Mozambican hero Samora Machel and later stepson of Nelson Mandela, Ntuane Machel.

Also with the first computer I ever touched in my life. In Pemba, there was no internet or television (handwritten letters took weeks to reach Uruguay, thanks to which I ended up marrying a former architecture colleague), but the encyclopedias on discs already hinted at what the world would be like in the coming century. Since then, Windows has not made any innovation, apart from annoying updates.

In this new world, I thought, every individual, from any corner, would be able to access the most important libraries in the world, and people would be able to decide in monthly or weekly referendums what to do with each project, with every proposal for their country and the world. We were not wrong about the libraries.

It's true that we also published a dark suspicion: the idea of a radical democracy, of an advancement of freedom as equal-freedom and not as the freedom-of-some-to-enslave-others, could be suspended in favor of its opposite: the progression of a tribal, nationalist mentality as a natural reaction.

Let's jump twenty years. Let's take a look, for example, at the logic of the development and growth of social networks, the legacy of a century of technological progress of humanity, hijacked once again by the powers that be. Their logic is the logic of business, of profits at almost any cost.

How are these profits generated?

By capturing attention, often to the point of alienating the individual, who becomes an addicted consumer who believes they are free.

How is consumer attention captured?

Not through big ideas but through simple and powerful emotions.

What are those simple and powerful emotions?

According to all studies (from Beijing in China to Harvard), negative emotions like anger, rage, and hatred.

What do these emotions produce?

Viral explosions. The *virality* of an event indicates the success of any interaction on social networks and is highly valued by honorary consumers and their ultimate beneficiaries, the investors.

What are viral phenomena good for?

Increasing users and hijacking consumer attention. That is, economic profits. But economic power and political power sleep together every night.

What is the political effect?

In a complex and diverse world, this effect can benefit any ideology, whether right or left, but the logic of the process and statistics indicate that the right is the primary beneficiary.

Why?

First, because all major social networks are products of megacorporations. Every private company is a dictatorship (in democracies and dictatorships alike). Neither the "virtual community" nor the consumers nor the citizens have a voice or a vote in how they are run. Much less in their algorithms and their economic profits. Every big business exudes its own ideology. Their ideology is necessarily conservative, right-wing, from the most primitive capitalism to neoliberalism, libertarianism, and all pro-capitalist fascisms. Just as the left developed within the culture of books, the right has reigned in more mass media like radio (Germany), television (the United States), and now, social networks.

Second?

The proven fact that hatred and anger reign on these platforms benefits the far right more than the far left.

Is there no hatred on the left?

Yes, of course, just as there is love on the right. But what matters here is considering the state of the overall climate. A leftist group, let's say a revolutionary group that takes up arms, like the enslaved Blacks in Haiti during the 1804 revolution, can use hatred as a tool of motivation and strength. But hatred is not usually the ideological foundation of the left, whose main banners are "equal freedom," that is, the vindication of groups they consider oppressed or marginalized by power. The hatred of class struggle is a tradition of the right; Marxism merely made it conscious. It is not the same to fight for equal rights for Blacks, women, gays or the poor as it is to oppose this struggle as a knee-jerk reaction to the loss of privileges of race, gender, social class, or hegemonic nations, in the name of freedom, homeland, civilization, order, and progress. That is hatred as a foundation, not as a tool.

Is there a difference between different hatreds?

Hatred is one and the same, it is a sickness, but its causes are multiple. The hatred of slaves for their masters, of the

exploited for their bosses, of the persecuted for their governments, is not the same as the hatred that radiates and spreads
from abusive power. The slave hates their master for their *actions*, and the master hates their slaves *for who they are* (an
inferior race). In the same way that no one with a minimum
of culture would confuse machismo with feminism, in the
same way one cannot confuse the patriotism of the revolutionary who fights against the colonizer with the patriotism
of the colonizer who fights to exploit the corrupted people.
In one, patriotism is vindication and the pursuit of equal
rights, of independence, of equal freedom. In the other, it is
the assertion of special rights based on nationality, race, religion, or any other aspect of intellectual provincialism.

What are the consequences of this electronic business?

Social media expresses the desire for war without the
risks of war. Until real war becomes present. This need for
confrontation, for channeling frustrations through rhetoric
and aggressive body language (the disheveled leader, proudly
obscene, calculatedly ridiculous to provoke more negative reactions) is typical of the far right on these platforms. Differently, the more formal right of neoliberalism preferred the
labels of aristocracy. Once all their policies, economic plans,
and social promises failed, they turned to the circus of the far
right, to body language rather than serene dialectical debate.
The culture of books, where the traditional left was educated
since the Enlightenment, is replaced by the culture of social
media of the right, where immediacy and knee-jerk reactions
reign and dominate. Aggression, anger, rage as expressions

of massive individualism (not the individual) become uncontrollable and, as if that were not enough, they become effective in the struggle to colonize semantic fields, truth, and the political power of the moment.

Little Red Riding Hood turns a thousand years old

In politics, as in the rest of the market, there are two fundamental engines: fear and desire. Especially in a culture based on consumption and a mercantile and success-driven system, often presented as if it were a natural organism governed by a single law, the Law of supply and demand. This same culture feeds on the idea that both, the market and its First Law, are logical, abstract, and universal expressions; not a system and a law regulated and directed by a hegemonic ideology and its different local policies. But every dominant social system is based, in turn, on the exploitation by power of the most primitive emotions of human beings.

Art, albeit with a different purpose, is also full of works that combine these two powerful engines of psychological and social life. The most raw examples are found in fairy tales, in stories about mysterious beings on every continent. Not by chance, the areas of the brain that trigger these two deep emotions are located almost in the same neural neighborhood.

In ancient Greece, this fear-desire impulse was illustrated with satyrs. A thousand years later, one of the oldest surreal stories, later considered as tales for children (long before the Brothers Grimm), is that of Little Red Riding Hood. As in a dream, this story (especially in its original versions before Disney sanitized it with Protestant moralizing) mixes sex, cruelty, mystery, deception, and death in ways as implausible as they are powerful, as proven by the tale's age in its written Latin version: in 2023, the innocent Red Riding Hood will turn a thousand years old, surviving the danger of the wolf in the forest and the house in the countryside.

But of the erotic pair fear-desire, only the first term represents the moralization of power to repress the second pair, which leads to temptation and the breaking of prohibition, the fruit of Eden. Repression and security are confused, just as fear and desire are confused in love or violence. Prohibition (the written one and the one internalized in self-repression) represents civilization, the law, civil, moral, or religious (*Critique of Pure Passion*, 1998). For these same reasons, fear is the visible face of the moon. On the other side lies desire, the need for transgression, for change.

Fear and desire also fill crime novels, mystery stories, commercial films, and even art-house cinema. Crimes, rapes, Beauty and the Beast, vampires sinking their teeth into the sensual neck of a defenseless woman… Without even going back to ancient Greece or the Renaissance, with its sexual stereotypes: rational men had tiny penises, like Michelangelo's David or Adam, while the dangerous and lazy satyrs of the forest (Dionysian fantasies, irrational) were depicted with donkey-sized phalluses. The same perception is found in the

letters of 19th-century white slaveholders, fearful that the liberation of black slaves would lead to the mass rape of white
women, when the reality indicated the opposite: not only did
black men suffer under the whip and the rifle, but rapes were
perpetrated by white masters and bosses against their black
slaves or servants, often minors, as was the case with the
Founding Father of American democracy Thomas Jefferson
and practically all the other honorable slaveholders from
Canada to Argentina. This pornographic fear-desire lynched
thousands of freed blacks after the Civil War in the United
States. Preventative—and legal—lynchings, as recommended by educator, feminist, and the first female senator
from Georgia, Rebecca Latimer Felton, who in 1898 recommended lynching blacks who won elections in North Carolina, claiming that the more educated and politically active
blacks became, the greater a threat they posed to the virginity
of white women.

The same pattern has been exploited for generations by
the powerful pornography industry, which thrives on "black
men with white women." That is, the fear of power opens a
safety valve in its own imagination. It is the tradition of *fes-
tivity* that breaks social rules and inverts the political order
once or twice a year, in contrast to the need for *ritual* that,
both in religions and in psychological tics, requires repeating
a certain order to feel some control over the uncertain future,
the unexpected, the feared, over what is truly uncontrollable.

According to Stephens-Davidowitz in his Big Data analysis (Everybody Lies, 2017), women consume twice as much

pornographic content featuring violence against women as men do. It hardly needs to be clarified that this does not imply any moral or ethical judgment, as it refers to psychological phenomena. One of the characters from my novel Crisis (2012), one of those characters detested even by their own author, summarized it thus: "In the end, after all this nonsense passes, the boring housewives, the proper feminist professionals want a man who humiliates them in bed. Only then do they recover their forgotten orgasmic capacities, desiring everything their education and morals abhor..." It's in the index of any Freudian book: in fictions, in folk tales, sex has been covered by a thick layer of symbolism, as in dreams. One must add: covered by the most visible and repressive term—fear.

This constitutive factor of fear and desire also has an explanation in the deepest prehistory. In 2008, Kent Berridge, a psychology professor at the University of Michigan (a member of the Biopsychology and Affective Neuroscience Laboratory), observed that dopamine, originating from the nucleus accumbens (central area of the hypothalamus) and motivating animals in their pursuit of pleasurable rewards (food, sex, drugs), is also responsible for the production of fear. Once the Michigan team inhibited dopamine production in mice, not only did their desire for rewards decrease, but so too did the anxieties produced by fear. The same team managed to identify the areas of the brain that are effectively related to fear and desire, and they found that these areas were separated by mere millimeters. Both fear and pleasure are responsible for the survival success of the species. A success, of course, riddled with conflicts, euphoria, and pain.

Once again, it is no coincidence that the powers of the moment, from classic authoritarian regimes to liberal democracies dominated by market ideology and a small number of feudal lords, owners of a few corporations, have exploited and amplified these two constitutional reactions of each individual for their own benefit. From political speeches to massive advertising campaigns and, more recently, the algorithmic dynamics of social media.

(Excerpt from the author's upcoming book, *Flies in the Spiderweb*)

When the Power Does the Leaking

In 2022, the FBI raided the Arabesque mansion of former President Donald Trump in Florida. He is accused of stealing hundreds of classified documents. Among the most shocking cases of the publication of classified documents after the "Pentagon Papers" are those of WikiLeaks' Julian Assange, the revelations by soldier Chelsea Manning, and former CIA and NSA agent Edward Snowden. However, the leaking of classified, secret information has long been a practice of the shadow powers in Washington, most of the time for propaganda purposes.

When in 2013 the leak of thousands of secret NSA documents proved that Washington was not only spying on citizens of other countries, President Barack Obama took to the press to deny it. On June 18, he stated: "What I can assure you is that if you are a citizen of the United States, the NSA cannot listen to your phone calls... That's by law." The president's words concealed a darker reality: the collection of trillions of metadata points is not classified as "direct listening" but rather as the gathering and storage of who made a call, to whom, at what time, and from where. By combining three or four of these events, the personal stories of each individual emerge on their own: psychological issues, unwanted pregnancies, debts, visits to pornographic websites, donations to unions or activist groups, and any other normal occurrence in the life of any citizen who has never broken any law but whose information can be used against them when necessary.

In 2012, Washington warned of the possibility that Chinese telecommunications companies, Huawei and ZTE, could be "violating U.S. laws," while at the same time the NSA was installing spy chips in routers and computers that U.S. companies exported to various countries. The routers exported by Cisco, for example, were infested with spyware, likely without the company's knowledge, as this practice was (or is) carried out by intercepting equipment ready for export and inserting bugs capable of taking over entire networks in other countries. The NSA also installed back doors in the computers of millions of Americans, intercepted servers, computers, and phones of tens of millions of Americans to collect and store their personal data. In the case of U.S.

companies producing in China, the law they follow is not Chinese law but U.S. law. This is why the restriction of the independence of foreign companies, such as Chinese ones, often falls under a kind of "extraterritorial jurisdiction" of Washington's justice system, as happened with Huawei in 2018.

The publication of the documents that proved the NSA's spying on nearly all U.S. citizens also revealed that this super-secret agency also handed over this data to the Intelligence Corps unit of the Israeli military, while complaining that Israel was not reciprocal but, on the contrary, was spying on U.S. citizens, defining Israeli intelligence services as "one of the most aggressive espionage operations against the United States." A leaked document states that a NIE (National Intelligence Estimate) places Israel as "the third most aggressive foreign intelligence service against the United States." Two years after these revelations, in 2015, Israeli Prime Minister Benjamin Netanyahu denied a report by the Wall Street Journal, leaked by the Obama White House.

When that same year, 2015, a report from the United States Senate revealed that the CIA had not only tortured innocent suspects at the illegal prison in Guantánamo but had also lied to the Senate and the White House, the CIA itself leaked part of its own secret documents to create the Public Opinion narrative that torture ("enhanced interrogation") had somehow been effective in keeping the country free from terrorist attacks. Something that was proven false, though no investigative commission is needed to realize that none of the major historical events were ever detected "in time" by "intelligence."

On page 401 of the same report, it concludes that *"the CIA leaked classified information to some journalists about its still-secret Detention and Interrogation program, which was later published."* The goal was to polish its image. The Assanges and Greenwalds of power were never pursued or brought to justice or before any tribunal. For example, "as an internal email states, the CIA _____ never opened any investigation into Ronald Kessler's book The CIA at War, even though it contained classified information... The legal advisor John Rezzo wrote that this decision was based on the CIA's relationship with writer Kessler having been blessed by the Agency's director. Another example is when CIA officials and members of the House Permanent Select Committee on Intelligence observed that an article written by Douglas Jehl in the New York Times contained a significant amount of classified information." Despite the illegal and privileged access to secret information—unsurprisingly—the same Senate committee concludes that "both Kessler's book and Jehl's article contain false claims about the effectiveness of the CIA's interrogation program." Before polishing his articles, Jehl provided a copy to Agency agents, even assuring them that the text emphasized the virtues of the techniques of the secret "enhanced interrogation" program. Ronald Kessler did the same in 2007 for another of his books: not only did he deliver the draft to the CIA but also included the changes and criticisms the agency had returned. (John Barron's bestseller,

KGB: The Secret Work of Soviet Secret Agents, also received
CIA funding and promotion.)

The list of achievements detailed by the two journalists
(capture of terrorists, prevention of attacks) was proven false.
But the Agency's propaganda machinery needed *"to make
'our story' public to create public opinion and in Congress"*. As
early as April 2005, the Agency had selected convenient information to prepare the officials who were going to be interviewed by journalist Tom Brokaw of NBC News about the
Interrogation Program in secret prisons abroad. Later, it
would become known that the *Dateline NBC* program not
only contained classified information but also invented stories about CIA achievements in capturing terrorists that
weren't even recorded by the Agency itself. According to the
director of the Counterterrorism Center, Phillips Mud, if the
CIA wasn't able to sell itself well to the public, Congress
could "limit our authorities and mess with our budget; we
have to make it clear that what we're doing is a good thing;
we need to be more aggressive out there: either we tell our
version of the story, or they'll eat us."

To a large extent, the CIA's competition with the FBI
and the mutual theft of authorities and credit is based on professional jealousy and an old struggle over budgets, despite
sharing the same political and geopolitical ideology of dom-
inating the always dangerous "others below." In an email on
April 15, 2015, to several CIA lawyers, an officer expressed
concern over this Agency practice of leaking classified information. No response is known.

It is known that the CIA destroyed the videos it had recorded during torture sessions, just as, after some time, it typically burns classified documents that, if leaked by more independent individuals, would not leave a good impression of the machinery, and the specter of budget cuts might come knocking again. The same Senate committee report, in its appendix data, compared the CIA's statements to Congress with the agency's own documents and concluded that its agents lied to legislators and to the public. Naturally, with no legal consequences and barely grazing or passing like a swallow through the conscience of Public Opinion.

What is the fate, the use that future governments, future paranoids, and future Artificial Intelligence analyses will make of those trillions of personal data points from hundreds of millions of citizens? For me, the answer is inevitable if we continue the same logic of individual espionage and the manipulation of collective truth: in the not-too-distant future, DNA analyses and psychological diagnoses of individuals will be used to classify people. For example, those diagnosed with "Oppositional Defiant Disorder" (ODD, or, as it is cynically reinterpreted in psychology, "Disorder of the Craving for Freedom"), will automatically be harassed and marginalized, not only in their political prospects but also in their employment opportunities.

As if that weren't enough, espionage systems have the capacity to search for information in all those files we thought we had deleted from the cloud and even from the hard drives of our private computers. This information has been illegally leaked by dissidents; however, we also know that the same secret agencies, including the FBI, have practiced mass extortion by allowing the public to know about the massive surveillance they conduct (something we might call the "strategy of alien paranoia"). This not only creates public self-censorship but also private self-censorship and, beyond that, censorship of thought, as in the darkest moments of the European Inquisition.

We need more autistics

During one of those colleague gatherings with the occasional stranger, the kind where (I've been told and read in the memoirs of retired manipulators) secret agents often go with a glass of whiskey in hand to discuss culture, a gentleman from Texas, an enthusiast of Central American history, asked me my opinion about Julian Assange and Edward Snowden. They know that few professors resist the temptation to give radical answers when someone delves into their areas of expertise. It also wasn't hard to deduce that in recent months I had bought several books on the subject, aside from my research at the National Archive. In just a few minutes, the man with the purple tie had reached the predictable point:

"Have you noticed that all of them have some psychological problem? Assange is a womanizer. The former agent Snowden is happily married, but he didn't even finish high school, despite his notable intelligence. The soldier Bradley Manning, later

Chelsea Manning, revealed herself as a woman trapped in a man's body. Glenn Greenwald fell in love with a Brazilian man and moved there... I'm not saying being homosexual or transgender is bad, only that it's a common factor they all share. What does this psychological pattern mean?".

"No, but..." At that moment, I remembered the persecution of blacks, gays, and lesbians implemented in the United States by Senator Arthur McCarthy and the infamous FBI director, Edgar Hoover, during the Cold War, considering that blacks and homosexuals were prone to betray their country and their religion by sympathizing with the communist causes of justice and equality.

In 2019 and beyond, Brazil's president, Captain Jair Bolsonaro, repeatedly referred to Greenwald with references to his sexuality ("Do you burn the donut?") as a way to personally and ideologically discredit him, to which the American journalist responded by observing the president's obvious anal fixation. After Snowden's revelations in 2013, Greenwald and his project The Intercept were also key in exposing the corruption of the Brazilian political system, from the corrupt anti-corruption judges like Sergio Moro, who managed to imprison the then-favorite presidential candidate, Lula, to the most corrupt parliamentarians who years earlier had impeached Dilma Rousseff under allegations of corruption.

Some of the most common labels applied to inconvenient dissidents like Julian Assange, Chelsea Manning, and Edward Snowden are "narcissist" or something related to a disability. Bob Schieffer, the star journalist of CBS (ironically, on a program titled "Face the Nation"), tried to discredit Snowden's revelations by dismissing him as a "young narcissist who thinks he's smarter than all of us" and comparing him to the risks Martin Luther King took, who stayed in the country after breaking the unjust laws of his time. To continue weaving the traditional media web, the powerful Business Insider headlined: "CBS's Bob Schieffer destroys Edward Snowden in 90 seconds." Edward Snowden and Glenn Greenwald (the journalist who published the documents leaked by Snowden) were repeatedly branded as "cowards" and "traitors," one for fleeing to Hong Kong and the other for moving to Brazil. The veteran CBS journalist failed to mention that Martin Luther King was pursued by the FBI and ultimately assassinated, like most leaders of the time, by "individuals unconnected to power."

"*What does this psychological pattern mean to you, Professor?*" insisted the gentleman with the whiskey on the rocks, whom I had never seen before but who had clarified from the start that he wasn't a new professor.

"*To me, it means the world needs more gays*, more transsexuals, and more autistics," was the only thing I could think to say, more to get rid of that gentleman with such high self-esteem and feigned ignorance. It worked, for the moment.

A few years later, one of my most advanced students, who had overheard the conversation, dropped by my office to discuss details of the course she was taking and mentioned a study she had read on ethics and autism. The research, published in *The Journal of Neuroscience* in February 2021 by an international group of nine experts (*"Right Temporoparietal Junction Underlies Avoidance of Moral Transgression in Autism Spectrum Disorder"*), conducted an experiment with two groups of people, one composed of individuals classified under the "autism spectrum" and the other of people outside it, or, in layman's terms, "normal people like us." Both groups were asked to donate a sum of money to associations, one charitable (for the education of children and teenagers in Brazil) and another that permits animal cruelty (elimination of dogs and cats from the streets) in two different contexts: some donations made publicly and others anonymously. In one case, a personal economic gain was offered for supporting animal cruelty. The computational model revealed that the group of people with autism did not accept this personal advantage at the expense of others' suffering, even when selecting the best option anonymously.

We can infer that this study not only dismantles the idea of the weak moral contextualization of autistic individuals, which often leads them to become entangled in social problems, but also reveals the opposite: a moral sense superior to that of "normal people." That is, this normality would be nothing more than adapting to personal interests (corruption) and manipulating others' opinions, which ultimately values them as "successful people," even though they should be undergoing intense psychological treatment if not for a sick culture that protects, rewards, and applauds them.

These "normal people" are the ones in the economic and political power of countries. When David Miranda, Glenn

Greenwald's husband, was passing through England, the secret services detained and accused him of terrorism. A terrorist for being the partner of a terrorist, defined in the accusation as follows: "Mr. Miranda knowingly carries material whose disclosure would endanger people's lives. Additionally, the disclosure, or threat of disclosure, is designed to influence a government and is carried out with the aim of promoting a political or ideological cause. Therefore, this falls within the definition of terrorism."

When secret agencies decide on secret, deadly, and devastating attacks in foreign territory, aren't they endangering anyone's lives? When they plant articles or circulate false rumors, aren't they shaping opinion in mass media? Aren't they trying to influence any government through public opinion? Parallel governments are never labeled as terrorists, according to their own very elastic definitions of terrorism. It's the obvious way of thinking. They are in power; their powerful fictions are called reality and normality, not "mental problems."

The giant on a collision course with its past

During the Thanksgiving holiday of 2021, we returned to New York. My son had an idealized perception of the city from the time we came back to participate in a talk at the UN. I also have good memories of Manhattan. It's one of the few cities in the country where urban memory isn't murdered every day with new containers from Walmart, Target,

McDonald's, Chick-Fil-A, Dollar General, and a few other chains that sell the same things in different colors.

After dozens of bus and subway rides, a fairly accurate image of the people emerges. Above, *YouTubers who think they're smart repeating stupidities; a cold accentuated by the eternal shadows and the bad mood of its inhabitants. Below, people who should be receiving treatment in a psychiatric institution (a man threatening to commit suicide again; a homeless woman sleeping in the cold who refused a full Starbucks breakfast my wife brought her, saying she had already eaten); subway stations that leak (Parsons, Queens) or lead to dirty and dark tunnels (14th St., etc.). It's like living in a dystopian movie like Terminator or the series Beauty and the Beast (not by coincidence, both featuring Linda Hamilton). Nothing that a hundredth of the 14 trillion dollars spent on the war in Afghanistan couldn't have fixed.*

Before classes resumed in January, we toured the coast of Georgia and South Carolina. The friendliness of the southerners contrasts with the unfriendliness of New Yorkers. But appearances deceive. When I left the long shadows of Pennsylvania for Florida, despite the promises of gold and riches, the director of Lincoln University's program warned me: "Nobody leaves a position like this. Southerners will smile at you before stabbing you in the back." But the bubbles of American universities aren't much like the other bubbles in society. Another social divide that explains the obsession with the Union.

Different theories explain the American custom of smiling at strangers, stemming from their immigrant past when nonverbal communication was the first resource. This contradicts the smiling provincials of the south and the grumpy cosmopolitans of the north. To explain it, perhaps one should turn to the slave-owning and segregationist past and the Culture of Masks, about which I wrote extensively a decade ago.

In Savannah and Charleston, I took several photos of monuments honoring Confederate generals and heroes, but there were so many that I lost interest. In Charleston (the city that horrified Simón Bolívar in 1807 when he witnessed the slave trade firsthand, contradicting his admiration for the American Revolution), it's not uncommon to see giant 4×4s proudly flying Confederate flags the size of bedsheets, the only terrorist group that came close to destroying the country to save slavery and who now consider themselves the epitome of patriotism and freedom. Their main street is still named Calhoun, after the senator who, during the invented war against Mexico (to expand slavery, but in the name of freedom and civilization), declared in Congress: "Not even in our dreams would we have accepted integrating another race into our Union that isn't Caucasian. Ours, Sir, is a government of the white race, of the free race. To incorporate all of Mexico would be to incorporate a race of Indians and mestizos."

These were not just his ideas but the ideas of the entire white South and a significant portion of the North. An American tradition that inspired Nazism in Germany (according to Hitler) and American messianism, in symbiosis with economic and military power. The masters and the strong of yesterday are the corporations and military bases of today.

Now, ranging from several professors to Jimmy Carter, people have begun to warn of an impending dictatorship in the United States, as if we should accept the national myth that we live in the superior, exportable model of democracy. As if the country of masks and faith over reality has ever been anything very different. What is different is (1) a strong sense of frustration due to its own socioeconomic system, exported as a model of success, and (2) another lost war and the absence of a new, media-driven one to ease the deep internal divisions. And violence that is not exported, but consumed in the domestic market.

The latest Monmouth University poll reveals that a third of the population (75 percent of Republicans) believes that Joe Biden stole the 2020 election. According to millions of Americans, including representatives and senators, Donald Trump was the winner. No different from the slave-owning Confederates when they lost the war in 1865.

Trump didn't even win the popular vote when he was elected president in 2016. He received three million fewer votes than his opponent, Hillary Clinton (yes, which is worse). As was the case with George Bush in 2000, the electoral system, inherited from the times of slavery to benefit the Southern states, full of Blacks without the right to vote, turned into presidents two candidates who would never have been so in any other country where every vote counts the same.

The problem is not that Biden might have manipulated the vote count, which is almost impossible. The problem is that the electoral system is archaic and profoundly undemocratic. The sparsely populated, rural, and conservative states in the center need half a million votes to elect a powerful senator to Congress. States with a majority of Asians, Blacks, and Latinos need between ten and twenty million votes, and twice as many votes per elector.

As if that weren't enough, in the face of growing ethnic diversity, Jim Crow strategies have been revived, reminiscent of 1868 when Blacks became citizens: laws that make voting more difficult for minorities with the right to vote. Now, new laws passed in states like Texas aim to make voting more complicated for the poorest. The poor, who are often Black or Latino, though it's unclear whether they are more hated for being Black, Latino, or poor. Not to mention the old and now revived strategy of gerrymandering, where electoral district lines are drawn to nullify any minority in any district. (If you cut a vanilla cake with a chocolate center, each slice will have a majority of vanilla, but the chocolate will have zero representation.)

Over the past two decades, the South of the United States has developed more than the North, precisely as the country begins to perceive the decline of its empire. This decline, like every true crisis, will bring changes unthinkable years ago. The drama will lie in a combination of geopolitical power loss and a strengthening of this nation's roots, which are not democracy, as is often repeated, but racism and a messianic sense of moral superiority.

Professor Richard Hasen has warned that a "democratic emergency" is already here. They have in mind a kind of dictator reminiscent of a Banana Republic. It's not that something like this is impossible, but it's not necessary. The United States was never a full democracy, and the fanatics who deny reality and are willing to take up arms to "defend freedom" didn't emerge now but centuries ago.

Another old mask. Racial obsession hides the fact that white majorities are, in reality, economically marginalized. A handful of male, white billionaires have more than all their enraged defenders combined.

That Trump is the messiah of the impoverished working class is no coincidence.

The Great Rupture of the 21st Century

Professor Walter Scheidel, in his book The Great Leveler, showed, more than convincingly, that from prehistory to the present day, all socioeconomic systems known to humanity have tended toward inequality and ended in global catastrophes. The first point is quite obvious and we are seeing it today: those who have financial and economic power have inflated political power, which leads to a snowball effect. The wealthy and their corporations are the major donors to political parties and then write laws to their advantage. In 1971, a classic from political comics, The Wizard of Id, summarized it unsurpassably: "The golden rule is that he who has the gold makes the rules."

In 2013, the French philosopher Thomas Piketty wrote his acclaimed book Capital in the Twenty-First Century, where he argued that, to a large extent, the growth of inequality is due to the wealth of the rich (based on stocks and property) growing faster than the economy and the income of the rest, that is, faster than the wages of those struggling to survive.

But inequality is not just economic; it's also racial, sexual, religious, ideological, and cultural. For generations, societies have debated the meaning of *social inequality* and whether it is good or bad. One of the conservative hypotheses (since they never reached the status of theories) was to justify inequality as a *natural consequence* of prosperity. In a tribe or in antiquity, the differences were never as great as in our (proud) modern societies. From there emerged the idea that (1) prosperity stems from inequity or (2) inequity is a necessary and inevitable consequence of prosperity. "Never before have the poor been less poor than today," and we owe all of that to capitalism and the rich.

This demonstration of radical ignorance is the banner of *libertarians* and *neoliberals*, missionaries against government intervention (that is, their regulations and taxes) in the social and economic lives of nations. Ironically, they hold the U.S. as their ideological model, whose prosperity, like

Europe's, was built on slavery and the force of brutal imperial interventions (by governments and their secret agencies)
upon the rest of humanity. Nor do they consider that corporations are dictatorships, much like the feudal systems of the
Middle Ages and the more recent banana republics.

Pure myths. Where is it proven that prosperity comes
from the accumulated wealth of the rich? Why not see that
development and wealth are products of humanity, rooted
in the experience and accumulated knowledge of thousands
of years of human history?

Another of today's dogmas lies in a misreading of Adam
Smith himself, according to whom all social progress is based
on the ambition and selfishness of the individual. Hence
comes the social myth that progress and prosperity are based
on individuals' ambition to become millionaires, which is
why we shouldn't "punish success" with taxes. A popular but
cheap myth, if we consider that all progress, almost all technical, scientific, and social inventions recorded in history
(even in the capitalist Era) were made by people who weren't
thinking about the damned money.

Social myths do not come from the people. They come
from power. Yes, (1) the Industrial Revolution multiplied (2)
wealth and (3) inequality a hundredfold, but these three elements cannot be separated from the (4) brutal Euro-Ameri-
can imperialism. If South America had pillaged the rest of
the world for centuries, it would now be a model of progress
and development.

The fact that today the poor are less poor than yesterday is not proof of the virtues of capitalism, as humanity has been making progress for millennia, all of it at an accelerating pace. No technical or scientific progress is due to capitalism or capitalists. The millionaires merely hijacked it. Current corporate capitalism is a legacy of the slave system: in the name of freedom, it exploits those at the bottom, concentrates wealth, sanctifies the master-entrepreneurs, and demonizes the worker-slaves.

At this moment, capitalism is delivering nothing but existential problems, such as (1) the destruction of the planet through growth based on consumption and destruction, and (2) the deepening of social inequalities, which will lead to greater conflicts. Capitalism is exhausted, and the crisis lies in denying the socialization of human progress, which will become inevitable (after the collapse) with mass robotization and the development of AI.

Suggesting that inequality can be solved through charity is like fighting an infection with an aspirin. Instead of healing, the infection grows. The collapse could be avoided by a global agreement, but if common sense were not a scarce commodity, we wouldn't be drowning in an environmental crisis. The alternative is a global collapse, a dystopian scenario where all currently accepted dogmas, such as the value of the dollar or private property, are shattered. A collapse where there are no winners, just a definitive regression to the Middle Ages.

If in a town people were dying of hunger and someone decided to light a cigarette with a hundred-dollar bill, they would be labeled immoral. Well, that's the situation we're in today. In other words, we're at the first of three levels:

1) *Morality*: It is immoral for children to die of hunger in a hyper-rich and hyper-technological world. Basic needs being met would be the first step toward a humanist civilization.

2) *Injustice*: Next, there would be the discussion of the injustice of what each person receives and on what basis.

3) *Convenience*: a less relevant discussion is about the necessity or convenience of inequality. For many of us, equity fosters development and even the production of wealth. Growth as a prerequisite for any redistribution is a dogma created by those in power.

The super-rich are the enemies of humanity. Not only do they hijack wealth from the rest, not only do they monopolize politics in democracies and dictatorships, but they also keep the majority in a state of hypnosis through (1) major propaganda outlets, (2) mediums of distraction, toxic and fragmentary entertainment, and (3) by virtue of keeping millions of other humans in a state of need, like wage-slaves without the time to realize that the pirates are not their brothers or neighbors.

But a large part of humanity loves, admires, and desires the super-rich, just as slaves loved the masters who gave them a potion at the end of an exhausting day. The master and the potion were seen as a blessing, and the rebels as demons who wanted to turn the world upside down.

Eleven problems of our time

The real need for an independent Latin American way of thinking remains an old utopia, not because there is no intellectual talent in our continent but because all independent forms have been repressed and demonized since 1492. Since then, the continent has passed from hand to hand up to the present day, where the dominant, neocolonial market ideology suffocates any alternative, using the ancient and effective tactic of demonization, funded by financial corporations and propagated by the media that serve them and the fanatics who suffer under them.

Although in varying proportions, power has always been in the hands of a minority. If we consider social progress as the equitable distribution of power in a society, we can see that, at least in the last five hundred years in the West, all political, social, and economic progress has been the result of other minorities far removed from power. These minorities were criminalized, demonized, discredited, and suffered threats, executions, massacres, or simply the silence of the majority, complicit with power. Thus, while these minorities criticized and resisted the brutality of the slave system, not a few Blacks, Indigenous peoples, women, and the poor taught other Blacks, Indigenous peoples, women, and the poor to be good Blacks, Indigenous peoples, women, and the poor.

Now, not without paradox, Islamophobes are leading the West into the same process that Western powers produced in the Persian-Arab world, transforming secular and socialist countries into paradigms of religious fanaticism ("The Slow Suicide of the West," 2002). The theocratization of current politics is not limited to boasting that God votes for our political party and helps us win football championships, but extends to cultural conditioning (a product of indoctrination that begins in childhood) where the greatest intellectual merit is having faith at any cost. While this is unquestionable within any religion, it loses meaning when these same individuals step out of their temples and confuse their religion with their ideology and their church with their country.

For any science, even evidence is conditioned by new data from reality that corrects it. In a religion, exactly the opposite occurs: if reality contradicts our desires, too bad for reality. There is no institution or philosophy more radically denialist than a religion. I say this from a technical standpoint, initially without making any judgment. If this denialism is acceptable within a dogma or religious creed, we cannot say the same when it comes to the factual world.

Hence, for example, the new trend of denying elections without evidence and only when fanatics lose them. This happens around the world where this religious culture, matured in the slave-holding South of the United States, has spread, proving once again the neocolonial nature of a hegemonic center, in decline but still with teeth.

11 needs to consider:

1.   *A new democratic and ecologist paradigm, one that transcends consumerism and the dogma of the market.* To achieve this, it is urgent to limit corporate donations to politicians.

2.   *A universal right to truth and transparency.* Corporations that grow beyond a disproportionate limit of political and social power must be restricted in various ways, such as the inclusion of qualified representatives of the people to oversee the corporation's actions. These committees must have an international nature.

3.   *A radical reduction in the concentration of power amassed by private* and transnational corporations. There is no democracy or transparency in their actions when faced with overwhelming power.

4.   *Decentralization of power,* both for corporations and the countries that protect them with their gigantic military might.

5.   *Abolition of secret agencies* as executive bodies of parallel governments.

6.   *Revival of a neo-Enlightenment,* where the paradigm of the cultured individual and the struggle for equal-liberty is once again considered a fundamental element in the fight for truth and against the current neo-medieval fanaticism.

7.   *Need for effective democratization.* At the beginning of the European Renaissance, capitalism represented a form

of democratization, somewhat replacing the hereditary privileges of the nobility with the more impersonal value of money. But capitalism did not invent democracy nor even modern democracy. On the contrary, it used democracy when it could not destroy it. The democratization process in Europe began with the humanists in the mid-15th century, and there was likely a form of proto-democracy in the first three centuries of Christianity, when its members were persecuted immigrants and their communal way of life had first stimulated the idea of equality. For their part, Native Americans were not only less sexist than Europeans, but they also practiced various forms of democracy, tolerance, and diversity, like the Iroquois in North America, even before the arrival of the conquerors who massacred and corrupted them with an abundant racist arrogance that continues to this day. The corporate capitalism of the last centuries is the reproduction of the American slave system and the European feudalism it initially opposed.

8.   *Internationalization of basic rights*, not only in their declarations but in their implementation. The UN is a toothless dog, where the absurdity persists that, for example, for decades almost all nations in the world have voted against the blockade of Cuba, yet it remains in place with the vote of two countries. It is a necessary organization but archaic in its architecture, which must be restructured, for instance, by increasing the number of countries with veto power in the Security Council. Or by directly eliminating the discriminatory right to veto.

9. *Universal Basic Income*. Criticism of this proposal based on the promotion of idlers is arbitrary. Slackers have always existed in every social class. Although it is often repeated that the poor are poor because they do not work hard enough, we can understand that the rich are not rich because they work harder than the rest. Beyond merit, which exists in exemplary and exceptional cases, it does not explain reality: the capitalist system accumulates benefits in a pathological way, and once this process begins almost at random, there is no room for any competition. A billionaire and former president like Trump launched his own social network to compete with Twitter and failed. Mega-companies grow and monopolize a market until they die due to new inventions, none of which are the product of their owners, who are applauded as geniuses by the obedient masses. Universal Basic Income will not eliminate traditional wages or new ventures; on the contrary, it will empower them. Most creative activity has always been done for free or without directly thinking about profit. Universal Basic Income will not only enhance the creative forces of individuals but, by freeing their existence from a wage conditioned on obedience, it will also liberate them from their fear of demanding truth, justice, and more democracy, something the minority in power fears like death.

10.   *Decommercialization of information*. Almost all major technological inventions, scientific discoveries, and social progress were made by people who were not thinking about the economic profits of their effort. When they were not

developments of the state. Both radio and the Internet were not developed through private company investment. Both were hijacked (privatized) at their peak maturity: radio in the 1930s and the Internet in the 1990s. Information became corrupted when it turned into a product, especially a product serving the power of the moment disguised as *freedom* and *pragmatism*. Like in times of slavery, the freedom of the owner of money and the whip. Without falling into the temptation of state censorship (that's what the aforementioned control committees are for), world governments can do much if they decide to regulate (that is, reverse) the powerful market of public opinion. Even more if they coordinate efforts and achieve, for example, a union of Latin American nations.

11. *Investment in public education* and decommercialization of education. Reestablish a balance between the humanities and technical subjects. Return students to being learners rather than clients. The (1) commercialization of education, like (2) healthcare and (3) the commercialization of the media, has produced a commodification of life. In other words, a new form of voluntary enslavement, what until the 19th century was called indenture and servitude.

Universal Basic Income now

The parable *"Do not give a poor man fish but teach him how to fish"* is not only favored in social media memes and a tool of self-indulgence when one is a poor person who has managed to save three dollars (an employee or small business owner who believes they are part of Elon Musk's guild), but also another resource for the moralization of colonialist capitalism that never misses an opportunity to blame the poor for their misery.

Few know how to fish better than a poor person, but this should not be surprising, especially when those who secretly hate them publicly label them as lazy. Those slackers who build our homes, who grow and harvest our food under the scorching sun, those who clean the bathrooms of our universities and airports and to whom no one even says *thank you*. Those who work like slaves in essential jobs but cannot go to the dentist and must resign themselves to expressing their modest joys without teeth. Those whose children cannot see a psychologist or psychiatrist, much less buy the medications that keep them balanced until their brains mature at 25, and end up instead, at 17 or 19, in police reports, in jail, and in social disdain for having *chosen* a life of crime and violence. Those invisible, cursed poor, who keep our rich, proud, and rotten world running at the whim of the proud successes and stewards of the system.

Contemporary history shows that the most effective way to reduce poverty and the obscene social inequalities is by giving money to the poor. This, which elicits unanimous laughter, can be understood if one dedicates a minimum of time to reflection. Reducing poverty at any cost is the most economical thing for a society, the best development strategy and the fairest from any point of view. Poverty does not stem from a race, a syndrome, or a cultural deficiency. It stems deeply from the rules and a social order established by history and, above all, by the dominant classes that control resources, the economy, politics, and the narrative of their created and desired reality through the media.

Every time a government in Latin America proposed some agrarian reform or the nationalization of its natural resources, with few exceptions (such as the nationalization of Mexican oil in 1938), it always ended in a coup d'état promoted by Washington and major corporations. Not long ago, when the president of Bolivia, Evo Morales expelled the demigods of the IMF and proposed that the country take charge of its own business, he was accused of being a dictator. To make matters worse, his political party included the word socialism. The numbers of the economy and social reality proved the "ignorant and dictatorial Indian" right (I quote, because it is something I had to hear more than once from Bolivian visitors in my office at Jacksonville University), something those in power never forgave him for. The same could be said of Brazil's president, Lula da Silva, who between 2003 and 2010 lifted 30 million Brazilians out of economic misery and cut child malnutrition in half, by giving checks (baskets) to the poor.

But every time a leader from some country in the Global South (from the former colonies) proposes a redistribution of wealth for the sake of simple justice and development social, he is automatically demonized as a "socialist dictator."

Ironically, those countries or nation-states that most demonize this idea of resource redistribution are the ones that practice it the most. Consider Saudi Arabia and other ultra-
conservative oil-rich countries, whose inhabitants receive direct subsidies from the exploitation of their national resources, considered "common resources." Consider the case
of Alaska, the bastion of the American radical right. Its citizens receive a salary from their oil resources, just for living
there.

The Universal Salary proposal, discredited by neoliberals
and corporations, has been criticized as an idea that would
promote laziness. What we call lazy people are often individuals with special needs who have not been assisted by society
to achieve a fuller and more productive life. We have already
explained these inverse effects of the Universal Salary in another space.

This does not mean that "drones" have the same rights
as those who strive. (I am referring to the slackers of the
lower classes and not those of the upper classes, because no
one needs to rely on rights when they have privileges in
abundance.) The Universal Salary does not eliminate the
principle based on personal merit, nor the intrinsic characteristic of human beings whereby the overwhelming majority of any society tends to create and produce new things.
Assuming that human beings are driven solely by economic
interests and the unlimited accumulation of wealth is assuming a simplified and dehumanized conception of the human

condition. A condition that has been corrupted by the capitalist, mercantilist, and utilitarian culture.

The proposal of a Universal Salary has a contradictory and paradoxical antecedent. During World War II, Juliet Rhys-Williams, a politician from the Liberal Party (then the left in England), proposed a "negative tax" by which all those who had an income below a minimum subsistence line should receive a subsidy inversely related to their income. That is, if we consider a curve of ascending incomes and intersect it with a horizontal line defining a minimum subsistence level, all those who fall below the line should receive as much as necessary to reach the minimum, while the others should pay more the higher their income. In his book Where Do We Go from Here: Chaos or Community? (1967), the socialist Martin Luther King had foreseen the solution: "We must create full employment or create income. I am convinced that the simplest approach will prove to be the most effective: the solution to poverty is to abolish it directly through a measure now widely discussed: the guaranteed income."

This idea was taken up decades later by one of the ideologues of neoliberal capitalism, Milton Friedman, and by President Richard Nixon. Why this sudden gesture of tenderness, when others of the same ideological stripe, like the writer of polemical novels Ayn Rand, were proponents of moral egoism? Octavio Paz wrote that the right does not have ideas but interests. However, when occasionally someone who appears to be an intellectual emerges on the right, there is no shortage of capital or the machinery of major media to promote them. Rand had several declared admirers in politics, such as the influential Federal Reserve Chairman Alan Greenspan, one of the architects of banking deregulation that sowed various crises in the most powerful empire in the world.

Capitalism is dying. The biggest problem is that, like feudalism, it will agonize for many generations.

In the meantime, we can look ahead a bit to the 22nd century and start with the changes.

Libertarians and their narratives
The (political) struggle for the semantic field

In 1986, I returned to my childhood, to my passion for Leonardo da Vinci, my mother's sculptures, and mathematics. But after two years of chaos and irresponsibility, my academic discipline was destroyed. It took me another two years of disorientation to retrain myself and enter the university to study architecture. But the two previous years of "Scientific Orientation," according to the Uruguayan system, had left me with several experiences of failures and sudden successes at the end. As in other moments of my life, I felt I could wake up in a few seconds (I was surprised when, suddenly, at five years old, I could understand what a newspaper was saying; at 19, I discovered that integral equations weren't Chinese but clear and simple language like my mother tongue; at 20,

I realized that the fifty students who were going to listen to my explanation about the bending of a beam weren't going to murder me or anything like that).

For the purpose of this book, I must say that this intense experience at such a young age left me with an epistemological mark: the idea that what we call *truth* or valid *thought requires certain prerequisites, clear principles, like an axiom, premises, a hypothesis, a theorem, a proof, and a corollary. To give a simple example: the transitive property (if A is greater than B and B is greater than C, ergo* A is greater than C) is an irrefutable deductive exercise. From two observations, a third fact, neither present nor observable, is derived by simple logic. Years later, in various construction projects and already as a professional, I verified this contradiction between practice and theory. The theory was always right. What people called *practice* was nothing more than obscure theories trying to justify specific and modest results, never general ones.

However, once I left architecture (especially structural calculus and some math classes in public pre-university to supplement my meager salary) for the humanities, the first thing that caught my attention wasn't just the obvious fact that human reality is more dramatic and complex than scientific abstraction, but that the method of analysis is simpler and less reliable. Greater variables, lesser deductive rigor. This does not mean a renunciation of rational thought but rather the need for other intellectual tools; just as a chess game can be won by a supercomputer based on the pure calculation of probabilities, a human being must ultimately rely on their professional intuition. In general, I observed, with silent obsession, that essays often boiled down to A = A. In *Critique of Pure Passion* (1998), I noted that, at the end of all pure mathematical speculation, everything also reduces to A = A (except that the second A is full of variants, full of other realities represented by symbols). But in humanistic, essayistic reflection and analysis, that formula reduced to A is A. Using samples of reality, the author had to convince, rather than prove, that A is K and K is not N (C+ and C- in The Narration of the Invisible).

This "is" is evident and repetitive in authors like the Mexican poet and Nobel laureate Octavio Paz. Others, such as the Argentine writer Ernesto Sábato, perhaps because he held a doctorate in nuclear physics, leaned more on phrases like "therefore" or "for which reason." Of course, induction is the most common method in essays, while fiction escapes these rational bounds entirely: its truth has nothing to do with logic but with empathy and inner upheaval. Reflection in a novel, a short story, or a poem is far from rational and deeply rooted in emotional reflection, just as what we see in a mirror is a sensitive, not deductive, reflection of our face and, very often, of our inner selves.

Here's what matters most to us now: in social narratives, often "ideological narratives" or "political storytelling," the "is," the mathematical equivalent "=," dominates and reduces to a few slogans or clichés. If we add to that the hyper-fragmentation of postmodern and neo-medieval thought on social media, the parts do not need to be related ("A Ford *is*

an erection," "love *is* hate," "the homeland *is* God," etc.).).
The relationship stems from the same micro-narrative opera-
tion, that is, from dictation. ("What time is it, soldier?"
"Whatever you say, General.")

In early 2005, I defended my master's thesis at the University of Georgia, *The Narration of the Invisible*: A Political
Theory of Semantic Fields. Essentially, the study dealt with
the social struggle for narrative, for the control of truth
through the control of language (particularly *ideolexicons*, a
neologism added a year later) and as a result of various successes and defeats between power and the social groups that
oppose it. As an initial example and metaphor, I used a photograph that had deeply impressed me during my first year
in the United States: in 1959, a group of protesters in Little
Rock, Arkansas, marched with signs proclaiming "Governor
Fabus, Save Our Christian America" and "Race Mixing Is
Communism." What caught my attention was not the assertion on the second sign but its dialectical nature, its purpose,
and its social and historical effects. Not because it was an
oddity, but quite the opposite.

Here, the referenced "is" (*is*) appeared as a *connector* to a
supposed "proof" of a truth, which in fact reflected an attitude of "revelation" typical of groups whose intellect has
been trained from childhood in a church. There was no induction, no abduction, and certainly no deduction. Only a
dictation, a revelation, of the same epistemological category
as any religious revelation. A revelation that didn't even have
a sacred scripture to connect it (*religare*), as if religion had

freed itself from its own god to fulfill political purposes, to defend social interests more directly.

To summarize briefly, in my 2004 thesis, I sought to analyze and contrast, from this semantic perspective, different epistemological discourses, ranging from classics of the left like *The Open Veins of Latin America* by Eduardo Galeano to responses from the political right like *The Twisted Roots of Latin America* by Alberto Montaner, along with other European texts (Unamuno/Ortega y Gasset) and Latin American texts (Sarmiento/Alberdi). The result was clear: as in chess, in the social narrative, there was (and still is) a struggle between two opponents for control of the center of the board. A positive semantic field (C+) that must be defined as clearly as possible in its boundaries (what it is) and a negative semantic field (C-, what it is not). "Social justice is W, not Z". "Freedom is X, but not Y."

Now, to achieve success in this semantic struggle, another dialectical level is necessary: *valuation*. That is, "X is good; Y is bad." How does one win the battle of positive and negative valuation over positive and negative fields? By association. In the case of *"Race Mixing Is Communism,"* this involves two semantic fields defined at the moment, but with opposite valuations. The first term (*racial integration*) is the term in dispute. The second (*communism*) has already been defined and confirmed in its social valuation (it is negative). Therefore, it is necessary to associate the disputed term with the consolidated term so that the latter transfers its negativity to the former through the binding equivalent "is". ("Social Distance = Communism", 2020).

Everyone knows that, in this specific case, the struggle over the meaning carried out by this group (in a world dominated by capitalist ideology) that attempted to associate racial integration with communism failed. The damned Civil Rights groups of the 1960s achieved one of those rare, overwhelming victories of the underprivileged over the ideology and power of the privileged. Partial and reversible, like all things, true. But a victory nonetheless.

I need not elaborate further on this point, but I believe it is necessary to understand it in order to grasp the rest of this book, which deals with propaganda and the narrative domination of societies. It goes without saying that this semantic battle reproduces the historical struggle between power and justice, that is, in our time, between those who accumulate money and political power and those who organize from below.

From a dialectical perspective, this analysis is anti-Marxist in the sense that it does not directly link the material conditions of production (and consumption) with the values and meanings of a society. However, since I see ("the narration of the invisible") a reality consistent within this theory of semantic fields and the importance of the Linguistic War, and at the same time I cannot refute the Marxist reading (the *base* as defining the *superstructure*), I understand that both views are or should be complementary. But to attempt to develop a general theory that integrates both, I am too old.

It. Neo McCarthyism on the horizon

Years ago, in 2015, the Florida Senate approved carrying guns on public university campuses across the State. Even though nearly half of the students are on medication and not a few suffer from psychological imbalances, exacerbated by culture and the natural crises of youth, the wise elders of the senate decided that if everyone carries a gun, everyone will feel safer. Something about "the land of the free and the home of the brave," who don't dare travel abroad because they can't sleep without a gun under their pillow. Perhaps that's why, in every generation, hundreds of thousands are sent with military equipment and high technology to "those shithole countries."

In 2021, the same Senate passed a bill requiring students and professors to report any ideological tendencies of their professors. Contradicting a previous law that prohibits recording someone without their consent, the new law permits (encourages) the recording of professors' classes so that they can be reported (not to the public but to the authorities) for any "ideological bias" (*bias*). Of course, the ideology of others, not ours in power. It's no longer enough that the boards governing universities are not elected by students and professors; it's no longer enough that (as denounced by the "communist president" Eisenhower) major corporations direct much of the research through "generous donations" that university presidents beg for daily to build nice buildings and pay "salary increases" that don't even keep up with inflation.

More? This year, 2022, Republican politicians from Miami (among them, a former Cuban mayor and a Cuban representative from New York) have proposed creating an ideological police force, akin to the KGB, to detect and pursue those suspected of being "communists": "a new position in the State Department [to] combat communism and authoritarianism... [A] Special Envoy to Combat the Global Rise of Authoritarian Socialism and Communism would be inspired by a similar ambassadorial-level position at the State Department that was created in 2004 to combat global anti-Semitism."

They forgot to add that the project is inspired by McCarthyism and the ideological persecutions of the FBI since the 1950s: targeting figures like Chaplin, Malcolm X, Martin Luther King, Frank Teruggi, Noam Chomsky, John Lennon, and so many others.

The former mayor of Miami clarified to the press: "It is time for the United States to reaffirm its commitment to combat communism *and authoritarianism worldwide. As the leader of the free world, we must continue defending the universal values of freedom, democracy,* and peace." Seriously, it's no joke.

More? Recently, a bill has been proposed that would prohibit schools from discussing people with unusual sexual orientations, such as gays and lesbians. The bill is known as "Don't Say Gay" and would ban any mention of their existence, meaning Walt Whitman, Oscar Wilde, and Tennessee Williams would become suspects in any literature course. Alan Turing would be banned in any computer science course. Books with mass killings, sure. Princesses awakened by the prince's rescue kiss, sure. Beating one's chest because we are a culture that defends diversity and freedom, sure. Recognizing that different people exist and can have the same rights as us "normal" people, no. The only difference between these people and the Taliban in Afghanistan is that on this side there is still resistance: us and the dangerous lesbian communists.

Now, what's new? On April 19, 1950, the *New York Times* reported on Senator Joseph McCarthy's dogma: "in recent years, sexual perversion has infiltrated our government and is as dangerous as communism." McCarthy had convinced the famed FBI director, Edgar Hoover, to pursue all gays and lesbians, considered "a threat to national security." On April 29, 1953, President Eisenhower signed an executive order prohibiting all homosexuals from working for the government.

Hoover hired a trusted aide of McCarthy, Roy Cohn, to fire all homosexuals from the government and any other type of job or, directly, send them to jail for their crimes against morality. Cohn was homosexual, known to Hoover, assistant to McCarthy, and later lawyer for the real estate mogul Donald Trump, when he was accused of racism in 1971 and then in 1978 for preventing blacks from renting in his buildings. Roger Stone, strategist for Trump's presidential campaign in

2015, met Cohn working for Ronald Reagan's campaign. According to Stone, "Cohn wasn't homosexual. He just liked to surround himself with blond people and have sex with men. Gays are weak, effeminate. He was more interested in power." Hoover, the longtime FBI director, was also homosexual. His partner, Clyde Tolson, accompanied him, in secret, until his death. But beneath that power, thousands lost their jobs for not being heterosexual enough, since, according to them, gays and lesbians, like blacks, professed the communist ideology of equality.

Even today, citizenship tests in the United States continue to include the question, *"Have you ever belonged to the Communist Party?"* Not a word about the Nazi Party, the Ku Klux Klan, or similar fascists. Same goes for the new bill in Miami and other offspring of their own kind.

Now, how can one avoid looking at reality? Recently, several professors lost their jobs for citing historical documents that included the word *"negro,"* even though they were using it to denounce racial violence throughout history. Even serious researchers have avoided (*just in case*) writing that word in full in their books and opted for "N***." It doesn't matter that until recently Martin Luther King, James Baldwin, and Malcolm X used it in every speech.

More? In Tennessee, the graphic novel *Maus*, by Spiegelman, has just been banned because it includes some profanity and the drawing of a nude woman. The book is a classic in its genre, recounting the memoirs of the author's father, a survivor of Auschwitz. The same puritanism that in 1921 censored the original English version of Joyce's Ulysses.

More? Several states have passed laws to prohibit the review of official history, banning the study of what is known as "Critical Race Theory." This includes *The Wild Frontier*. Conservatives love to call any theory they dislike a "theory," like the Theory of Evolution. The Theory of creation in seven days wouldn't be a theory but a fact.

The strategy is clear: if no one talks about *it*, *it*, then it doesn't exist. As a result, *it* persists, as in the times of slavery, driven by the same will of the victims themselves. It's clear that power will always hate "the intellectuals." Their speeches, like those of Latin American oligarchs, were written by the CIA in the 1950s. Among these simple ideas, one was summed up by President Nixon: "I will never agree with the policy of reducing the power of the military in Latin America. They are centers of power subject to our influence. The others, the intellectuals, are not."

As always, all this garbage will find its way to Latin America in one form or another. After all, they remain colonies proud of their freedom.

The supervised freedom of libertarians

Florida Governor Ron DeSantis has banned 54 math books, claiming they include Critical Race Theory and new pedagogical methods that, according to him, "are not effective," such as Social and Emotional Learning (SEL). He didn't explain or discuss which paragraphs in math textbooks could be anti-racist but held a press conference in the style of denialist politicians: with furious obviousness about how the universe was created, morality, and the sex of snails.

The media and platforms create a psychological need, and denialist politicians sell consumers the drug that relieves them, a drug with every reactionary ingredient imaginable: security, immediacy, victimization. Some hallucinations are as old as the Theory of White Genocide, invented in the 19th century when Black people became citizens, almost human beings.

This politics of denial deepens and limits the discussion of identity politics (such as the denial of racism; the denial of the existence of gays and lesbians) silencing frameworks like the existence of class struggle and any form of imperialism itself. If it's not talked about, it doesn't exist.

This product sells so well that, as has happened for centuries, it's being exported manufactured to the colonies of the South. For example, just the name "libertarianism," now a banner for rising figures of the far-right in Latin America like Argentina's Javier Milei, is a literal copy of the "libertarians" who emerged in the United States as a reaction to the humiliating election of a mulatto as U.S. president in 2008. Like the Tea Party, these groups always justify themselves in a tradition taken from the so-called Founding Fathers. Even in Argentina and Brazil, the yellow flag with the serpent, symbolizing the union of the Thirteen Colonies, coiled around the motto "Don't Tread on Me," has been waved, though it seems more like a human excrement emoji. Also in Europe, Latin America, and even in Hong Kong, right-wing groups have proudly flown the racist and pro-slavery flag of the Confederacy.

Many Americans who proudly display this flag on their 4x4s are shocked when reminded that it's the flag of the only group that almost destroyed the country they claim to defend (the United States), with the sole aim of maintaining slavery and white privilege. Many don't even know this because in this country, raw history remains one of the most entrenched taboos.

It's not without irony that a conservative libertarian, Texas Representative and presidential candidate Ron Paul, acknowledged and condemned Washington's imperialist tradition and blamed it for the rise of Latin American leaders like Fidel Castro and Hugo Chávez. "We don't remember anything, and they forget nothing," he said in a debate. Because of this insistence, he was silenced by the mainstream press, and many of his followers (including some of my former students, who continue to be politically active) ended up voting for socialist Bernie Sanders.

The new label of "libertarian" was a well-known business strategy: when a company is drowning in debt, it declares bankruptcy, changes its name, and continues the same business. The same thing has happened with neoliberalism. Forced upon Chile with Pinochet and imposed by the force of international banks in dozens of other countries in the 80s and 90s, and more recently with Mauricio Macri in Argentina and Luis Lacalle Pou in Uruguay, it has always ended in painful failure, not only economically but socially. Naturally, failure for everyone but their class interests.

Libertarian and *neoliberal* are the same thing, but libertarians added the fury of Savonarola and Luther. It's the same difference between the calm sermon of a Catholic priest and the sweat-drenched rant of a Protestant pastor. Remember those polite young men with British accents who preached neighborhood by neighborhood, saving souls (especially their own) back in the 70s and 80s? Well, the seeds have borne fruit.

Contrary to the Founding Fathers of the United States, who insisted on separating religion from the state (a legacy of Enlightenment philosophers), libertarians have brought the *missionary* into government. In Brazil, they organized prayers in Congress; President Bolsonaro's wife herself is an influential pastor; in Costa Rica, the wife of a candidate "spoke in tongues" to support the electoral campaign; more recently, Deputy Milei argued in Congress against taxes by quoting the Bible: the Jews left Egypt to escape slavery and taxes, just as business owners are leaving Argentina today. The list is long and significant.

The politics of denial is the politics of frustrated success: "the right knows how to govern but is unlucky," which is why it always fails. This sense of frustration was a reason why so many millions of civilized Europeans supported fascism and Nazism a century ago. If we no longer see it coming, it's because we're already inside this suicidal absurdity.

As if all this fanaticism weren't enough, Governor De-Santis, like his Southern imitators today, insists that professors and civil rights activists indoctrinate youth. But what indoctrination is more radical than teaching to deny history in the name of God, freedom, country, and family?

What's more indoctrinating than telling children over and over that we are the champions of freedom? That we never invade to defend economic interests but, as Roosevelt and the slavers said, out of altruism, to bring freedom to Black countries that don't know how to govern themselves. What's more indoctrinating than denying the horrors of a history we aren't responsible for but adopt when we say "we" and then deny having done any wrong?

What's more radical than portraying the traditional oppressors of class, gender, and foreign ethnicities as victims?

What's more radical than Kipling's poem, "The White Man's Burden," the banner of the happy imperialist who carried the Bible in one hand and the whip in the other?

What's more radical and worse indoctrination than the politics of denial that allows old collective crimes to be committed as if they were new tribal rights?

What's more radical, dogmatic, doctrinaire, and hypocritical than filling podiums with speeches against "cancel culture," furious speeches about freedom, and as soon as they come to power, repeatedly passing laws banning saying this, discussing that, doing the other? The same hypocrisy of the

U.S. slaveholders who defended the expansion of slavery in the name of freedom, order, and civilization. No different from the Latin American dictators promoted by the Transnationals, heirs of the powerful Southern slaveholders.

This rancid right, rejuvenated through surgery, is so *libertarian* that it only prohibits something when those below threaten to obtain or retain some right. Always in the name of Law and Order. As Anatole France said, "The Law, in its majestic equality, forbids the rich as well as the poor to sleep under bridges, to beg in the streets, and to steal bread."

Peter Pan and the Power of Political Fictions

On Monday, February 7, 2022, Florida Governor Ron DeSantis, Lieutenant Governor Jeanette Nuñez, and the Attorney General attended a roundtable at the American Museum of the Cuban Diaspora in Miami. In his speech, the governor stated that comparing the suffering of Cuban children exiled during Operation Pedro Pan in the 60s with Central American immigrant children is "disgusting," because the former were fleeing communism.

The others flee capitalism since the 19th century.

Mr. Governor and White House aspirant: I regret to inform you that, beyond the in-house applause, you have once again repeated an old lie that fell apart long ago, even though fanatics continue to venerate it as a revelation of the Holy

Spirit. The same CIA agents admitted it. I know you'll ignore this, but the truth must find its way in somehow.

On December 26, 1960, the new Cuban government had initiated a program of educational reforms. Perhaps to avoid repeating the history of the coup in Guatemala six years earlier (instigated by the CIA thanks to the democratic opening of the eventually deposed president), they sought to teach young people how to use weapons. In the United States, conservatives do the same with their children, but it's not "indoctrination" but rather "fighting for freedom."

As conservatives in the U.S. do when they teach their children to call anyone in poor countries who fight for their rights or against Washington's interventions "communists," the revolutionary government at the time also aimed to teach their children songs against imperialism, which, both on the island and in the name of freedom, had begun before 1898. To make matters worse, many Cuban parents were concerned about the extremism of the new government's indiscriminate literacy program.

For decades, the books and newspapers of the Free World reported that children in Cuba's revolutionary primary schools "were forced to learn the values of the Revolution." It is assumed that in the rest of the world, children in schools and churches are free to think for themselves (except when they become young adults and reach universities; then they are "indoctrinated" by professors).

In 1960, on the Swan Islands, claimed by Honduras and occupied by the CIA, an unlicensed radio station was set up to broadcast propaganda to Cuba, with Cuban broadcasters arriving from Miami. Radio Américas (later presented as "The first democratic voice of Latin America") began spreading the rumor that the communists were going to forcibly send Cuban children to Russia.

Like in Orson Welles' radio episode about an alien invasion (put into practice during the successful coup d'état in Guatemala), panic immediately spread. 47 years later, in his memoir Trained to Kill, the Cuban CIA agent, Antonio Veciana, would proudly acknowledge: "Maurice Bishop [David Atlee Phillips] knew that I had been responsible for the fire at one of Havana's most famous stores, which cost the life of an innocent young woman, a mother of two. He also knew that I had been responsible for spreading the rumor that led to the exodus of thousands of Cuban children in Operation Pedro Pan, with the help of the Catholic Church, lying that they were orphans. He knew that it was I who nearly collapsed Cuba's economy with that rumor campaign aimed at sowing panic among the population."

But Veciana had learned from Phillips. In his 2017 memoir, he acknowledged that, according to the CIA agent who had recruited him in Havana, "modern wars are, above all, psychological wars; the goal is to twist public opinion." The strategies, of course, are more specific: "we must never leave traces of our actions; if this is not possible, we must always and under any circumstance deny any involvement in the events. Always. Even when the opposite is the most obvious.... If the interests of others align with ours, then they are allies; if they have no interests, they are tools; if they oppose our interests, they are enemies."

Antonio Veciana, as a bank employee for Cuba's richest man, the Sugar King Julio Lobo, had met twice with the new president of Cuba's National Bank, Ernesto Guevara, and, after some hesitation, had dismissed his request to recruit accountants and administrative staff for Cuba's new financial system following nationalization. From his retirement in Miami, Veciana defined Che as a fanatic of telling the truth at any cost.

But Veciana felt proud his entire life for having launched the historic plan, even without the initial approval of the CIA. He even managed to print thousands of pamphlets informing about a law that never existed. The effect was similar to that discovered by the propagandist and social manipulator Edward Bernays (having an authority on the subject say what you want everyone to think): in Miami, the priest Bryan Walsh announced that the Cuban government planned to separate all children aged three to ten from their parents to send them to Russia. The CIA took note and, from its clandestine radio station in Honduras' Swan Islands, began repeating the false story. Until it became dogma.

Father Walsh, through his Catholic Welfare Bureau, officially launched Operation Pedro Pan, with which Cuban parents, desperate over the rumor, sent their children to the United States. From December 26, 1960, until the Bay of Pigs invasion in April 1961, hundreds of children flew daily, unobstructed and without adult supervision, on Pan Am to Miami to be saved.

When the program was interrupted due to the Superpower's defeat at the Bay of Pigs, 14,048 children had already arrived in the United States. Some, nine or ten, were success stories for the media and the collective dream, according to the concept of success at the time. One would become the stepfather of the world's richest man, Jeff Bezos. Another would be Mel Martínez, U.S. Senator (a hero of the "English-only for children" proposal and "no amnesty for illegal immigrants"), irrefutable proof of the American dream and the freedom of the victor.

In 2007, Robert Rodríguez, one of these "unsuccessful" children, would denounce Monsignor Bryan Walsh to the Archdiocese of Miami for repeated sexual abuse against him and other minor refugees in Opa-Locka, Florida. The priest Mary Ross Agosta would accuse the accuser of "defaming a respected clergyman who saved the lives of fourteen thousand children." The complaint by Rodríguez and others against the same archdiocese was dismissed due to legal technicalities that are not applied in other states. In Florida, various monuments still today remember Monsignor Walsh with flowers.

Many children saved by Operation Pedro Pan from being separated from their parents by communism took years, decades to reunite with their parents. Some never saw them again. Because of communism, of course.

Drowned for not wetting their feet

At 12:20, that hour when students leave their classes and flood the campus parks for the first respite of the day, I was heading from one building to another to seclude myself in my office. At a bend of trees and plants where some usually rest from their less creative obligations, someone waved at me with a hand to beckon me closer. Two colleagues were having coffee at a small table and seemed to have been in the middle of a discussion. They are two colleagues and friends whom I love dearly, and who, for the purposes of these notes and to avoid any invasion of others' privacy, I will call Albert and Marie. Both are brilliant scientists, authors of recognized research in their fields.

It didn't take long for them to inform me of the topic that preoccupied them. It's in all the national media, especially after the war in Ukraine. Just last year, several congresses in the United States have passed laws to ensure that in public education, the history that critically mentions racism (Critical Race Theory) is no longer taught and to ensure that the existence of gays and lesbians isn't even mentioned. The excuses are for children, but they work perfectly, as the central role of the major media is to infantilize voters: "some white boys might feel uncomfortable when talking about slavery and racial discrimination" and "we must avoid sexualizing young people" when acknowledging that, in addition to love between men and women, there are other odd people who love equally, but the wrong person.

Albert and Marie were outraged and couldn't find an explanation for such a setback. The new laws passed by the Florida congress were ready to be signed by Governor DeSantis, the guardian of the people's morality blessed by God. Regarding the new McCarthyistic policies against journalists, teachers, and free thinkers, we already stopped at another bend a few weeks ago.

"It doesn't affect us because we're at a university," said Albert "and the government can't dictate our curricula. But how far are we going to go with this nonsense?"

"More or less, it doesn't affect us," I added. "For now. The fact that we're not high school teachers, nor gay, nor women, nor considered Black or Yellow is irrelevant. Who can really be free under the heavy burden of others' injustice? A few, you'll tell me. Not me. Injustice is everywhere, and most of the time it's unseen or deliberately ignored. Right here, for example.

"What do you mean?"

"At the last faculty meeting, we were informed that we'll be receiving students from Ukraine, exempt from paying tuition."

"Ah, yes. That question about whether we'd give the same benefit to young people from Yemen, Syria, or Palestine was really tough."

"I insisted again on Twitter, in case they decided to answer."

"Did they reply?"

"We've heard you, and stuff like that."

"Well, it's because you can ask those questions."

"Why me? Every time I do it, I find little support from people like you, who then end up agreeing with me but didn't say a word when the time came."

"It's because you can do it."

"I still don't understand."

"Because you're known in many places, and no one would dare to…"

"…ask for my resignation? Are they waiting for me to make a "mistake" to do it?"

"No one wants a scandal," Marie insisted.

"Every now and then, I see some students filming me with their phones when I talk about the CIA's responsibility in the destruction of Latin American democracies or about Washington's promotion of communism in Latin America and private Corporations through their long, century-long history of invasions and puppet dictators. Of course, if I were in Latin America, the functional oligarchy's enforcers would have already made me disappear. Here, it's still different. No one wants that kind of scandal in the center of the world, right? Trujillo did it in 1956, kidnapping Professor Jesús Galíndez from Columbia University, and Pinochet in 1976 with the terrorist attack that killed Letelier in Washington, but those are exceptions.

"The governor wants students to record us and denounce us for ideological tendencies."

"In your case, Albert, you don't investigate global warming. Relax. In my field of study, it's more complicated. Once I had to stop the class and tell them, 'Guys, you're wasting your time: everything I'm saying I've already said or published before. What you see is what it is. I'm not a coward hiding behind pseudonyms or spying on others' classes to report back to their bosses. I'm not a mercenary agent paid to ruin anyone's life. Everything I do, I do for the truth, the one no one wants to hear. For thirty years, I've been saying and publishing the same thing, no matter the consequences.' That hurts, doesn't it?"

"Has an extra actress ever been planted on you?"

"Once, a federal agent visited my office under the pretext of confirming job references I'd given for a student. I told him he could do it over the phone, but he insisted on seeing me in person. He showed me a badge without giving me time to read it. It was very ridiculous. They know they have to do more to earn the title of *intelligence*. And I know sooner or later I'll end up falling."

"How?"

"Haven't you noticed that dissenters often die of cancer in significant numbers? No?"

"Edward Said…"

"Frank Church…"

"Or uncomfortable leaders down South. Well, I've said it before, as a form of protection. Once you anticipate their plans, you force them to change and be more creative. One might think you're becoming paranoid, but what's more paranoid than the reality of McCarthyists? Just delve into history, and there's no doubt left. No, I'm not well-known or anything. I live exposed, unprotected. Intellectually, I'm a homeless person. And when it comes to speaking out against injustice, not everyone who agrees gets their feet wet. Not even in a faculty meeting. Like you."

"Well, Jorge, you have to understand. It's not always easy. Besides, the fact that some people prefer not to speak up about certain topics doesn't mean they agree. They have the right. Nowadays, everything is so politicized that if someone comes to talk to me about the Super Bowl instead of the war in Ukraine or the victims in Palestine, I'm grateful. That doesn't mean I agree with any of it, but I can't handle everything."

"Well, you've just answered your initial question. Do you understand now why we're immersed in Neomedievalism? The obligation not to discuss the present, and not even the racist past of this country, the prohibition of recognizing or speaking about different sexual orientations not accepted by the Holy Office, isn't a rain of toads that fell yesterday. Behind the governor and the legislators in Congress, there are millions who think alike: 'Oh, no, politics is toxic, better not get into those issues,' 'I can be a good person and not protest when someone's human rights are violated...'"

After all, there will always be someone who takes the risk, and when things go wrong, we'll join in lynching the dangerous individual.

Marx did it

At the University of Florida, United States, they renamed the Karl Marx study room. Now it's called Room 299. At least for now, because considering the new laws that prohibit discussing the racist history of this country in schools, perhaps in three years they'll inaugurate a room named Azov Battalion to celebrate the 160th anniversary of the Ku Klux Klan's founding, inspired by Adolf Hitler and never banned in this country, as it represents a very (North) American tradition.

Those who proposed removing Karl Marx's name did so in reaction to Russia's invasion of Ukraine. Since Marx was born in Prussia, that sounded like Russia, not Germany. Furthermore, today's capitalist Russia must be Marxist because it is part of the former Soviet Union. A journalist from Gainesville supported the decision by stating that Marx had been responsible for "millions of people who died as a direct result of his ideas." A classic cliché (coined by CIA's Cuban agents) that also defines Che Guevara as a "murderous monster" and omits the hundreds of thousands massacred as a more than direct result of CIA plots that created the Che in Guatemala.

Now, claiming that Marx is responsible for the deaths caused by some communist governments is like saying that Jesus is responsible for the deaths caused by Christianity (which, by far, were many millions more than those of communism), that Adam Smith is responsible for the millions of deaths caused by capitalism (which, by far, were many millions more than those of communism), and so on with everything else.

The hundred million deaths of communism

On February 28, 2023, the Republican representative of the Cuban exile in Miami, María Elvira Salazar, presented a proposal to condemn "the crimes of socialism." The well-known Miami radio and television station José Martí, which since 1983 has produced ideological propaganda in favor of the freedom of capitalism and private enterprise with government funds exceeding 30 million dollars annually, headlined: "US House of Representatives approves resolution denouncing the horrors of socialism." Of the horrors of capitalism, several times more tragic, not a word.

But we will talk about them, even though we don't have the millions of dollars to prove we are right, just humbler data and arguments.

In *The Wild Frontier* (2021), we paused at Operation Mockingbird (*Mockingbird*), one of the most secret and, at the same time, most well-known plans of the psychological and cultural war organized and financed by the CIA with millions of dollars during the Cold War, which included not only articles with fake news in newspapers but also the promotion of mediocre yet convenient books and the "neutral and devastating" criticism of those that didn't serve as propaganda. We also briefly touched on hints and the few but compelling leaked evidence of an even more extensive and aggressive continuation of the same practice, such as in film and television, in earlier chapters of this book.

Let's look at one of the most promoted and viralized cases of the 1990s, such as *Le Livre noir du communisme*, published by the former Maoist Stéphane Courtois and other academics in 1997. We won't dwell now on the well-known psychology of the convert, because it's unnecessary. The book was a kind of *Manual del perfecto idiota latinoamericano* but for the first world and with much more influence, even though both were massively promoted by the global press.

This book is the source of the endless social media posts about "the hundred million deaths of communism," although its own authors estimate a lower number, between 65 and 95 million. Other scholars and specialists in the 20th century and the topic (its authors are not among them) noted that Courtois listed any event involving a communist country and took the highest figure in every case.

For example, the deaths of World War II are attributed to Hitler and Stalin, when it was the latter who was primarily responsible for the defeat of the former, and it was the former, not the latter, who caused that tragedy. Furthermore, *Le Livre noir* concludes that Stalin killed more than Hitler, without considering the reasons behind each tragedy and attributing part of the 70 to 100 million deaths in World War

II to Stalin, when one started the war and the other ended it. The twenty million Russian deaths are attributed to Stalin.

Specialists in the Soviet era estimate Stalin's responsibility at something over a million deaths (forced labor in Gulags), which is a horrific figure, but far from what is attributed to him and even further from any of the massacres caused by the other capitalist superpowers, former allies of Stalin. The deaths and presumed deaths from hunger are included in the anti-communist equation, but not the millions of lives saved from hunger and disease by the Soviet revolution. The intentionality of the 1932 famine in Ukraine, known as the Holodomor, remains disputed among historians. Several facts are frequently omitted from the discussion. For example, much of the initial data was fabricated by the American press mogul William R. Hearst, an anticommunist and pro-Nazi figure, inventor of Yellow Journalism and the myth of the sinking of the Maine, an event that triggered the long-desired war against Spain in Cuba in 1898.

The Stalinist government carried out the most impressive modernization and economic improvement in modern history after post-Mao China. Not only did it industrialize agrarian and impoverished Russia, but in twenty years, it doubled per capita income. In the early 1920s, the life expectancy of the Soviet population was 26 years. By the end of the 1950s (famine and Gulags included), it had reached 68 years. In the 1970s, it declined and recovered by the mid-1980s. Between 1990 and 2005, it fell from 69.1 to 65 years. Simply multiplying thirty additional years of life by the millions of people who lived during that period gives an idea that, in terms of lives and deaths, the policies of the dictator and the Russian revolution had a decidedly positive impact. We won't discuss here, as it is a separate topic, his repressive policies, such as sending dissidents to forced labor camps.

The "100 Million" narrative also fails to mention that after World War II, while brutality decreased on the other side of the Iron Curtain, it increased in the backyard of the United States. John Coatsworth, in his *The Cambridge History of the Cold War*, highlights a verifiable fact: between 1960 and 1990, "the number of political prisoners, torture victims, and executions of nonviolent dissidents in Latin America far exceeded the number of victims of the Soviet Union and its satellites in Eastern Europe."

Let's briefly look at a classic example (not the first) of a capitalist tragedy attributed to "natural causes." Once again, the abstraction of coercion inaugurated by the capitalist market provides the perfect alibi to avoid taking responsibility for tragedies while claiming credit for any social progress.

Ireland was the first colony of English capitalism, in the sense that it imposed the new rules of fluctuating rent tied to the market and stock exchanges. By 1840, Ireland had a population of over eight million. In 2023, it barely reaches seven million, despite the fact that, since then, all European countries have multiplied their populations several times over. Just as traditional historiography attributes the deaths from famine in Ukraine or China to communism, without considering any natural phenomena, it also, but conversely, attributes the catastrophe in Ireland to a potato fungus. The cause of nearly two million Irish deaths and many more emigrants was not a fungus but capitalism, something that is not very hard to explain.

The blight originated in Mexico and spread from the United States to Europe. Neither those countries nor the rest of Europe suffered famine due to potato shortages, simply because they had more diversified agriculture.

Since the beginning of capitalism, Ireland was the first imperialist laboratory for England before projecting itself onto its overseas colonies, just as the banana republics in the U.S. backyard were the laboratory for the United States before venturing into the rest of the world. Just as the privatization of land had liquidated communal lands in England in the 16th century under the enclosure system (*enclosure*) and turned peasants into renters and the dispossessed, in Ireland this system was imposed to transfer a large portion of cultivable land to landlords. Just as Western empires would promote monoculture in their colonies (gold, silver, sugar, tobacco, cotton, bananas, coffee, diamonds, copper, meat, leather, wool, tourism, immigrants) in their protectorates and satellite republics, Ireland had become a European colony with the Peruvian potato as its monoculture and the main source of calories for its population.

Even before the appearance of the blight, various observers had denounced the dire living conditions of Irish peasants, who made up the majority of the population. Most of the peasants' earnings went toward paying rents, which were defined in England and, supposedly, by the sacred Law of Supply and Demand dictated by the market.

When the famine crisis erupted, the London government claimed that the problem would be resolved by the magic of the free market, while landlords exported other products produced in Ireland, such as meat and milk, to meet the needs of the market in England. William Smith O'Brien of Limerick had already noted in 1846: "What is most outrageous is that people are dying of hunger in the midst of plenty." A story all too familiar to other colonies, like India or Bangladesh.

Not by coincidence, the official in charge of the Irish crisis, Sir Charles Trevelyan, was a returnee from the brutal administration of India and, not by coincidence, initiated anti-Irish racism, which would cross the Atlantic behind its own victims. Trevelyan was a fervent advocate of the free market and laissez-faire, a convenient policy or superstition for the few, which survives to this day in the 21st century. Like almost all free-market fanatics, by some mystery of Creation, he turned to God to explain anything complicated: once his method failed to resolve the crisis, he blamed the Irish, stating that "the judgment of God sent this calamity to teach the Irish a lesson."

While the executions of nearly a thousand collaborators of Batista's regime in revolutionary Cuba are tirelessly mentioned in all media, the more than 100,000 executed by the Christian and pro-U.S. regime of South Korea are ignored. On July 26, 1950, in No Gun Ri, American soldiers of the

Seventh Cavalry Regiment massacred 300 South Koreans, claiming they feared that among this miserable line of refugees there might be some North Korean soldiers. Decades later, this massacre was acknowledged by Washington and forgotten by nearly everyone except revisionist historians. In 2009, based on declassified documents in the United States, the *Truth and Reconciliation Commission*, estimated that, apart from American bombings, the South Korean regime carried out summary executions that reached the figure of 150,000 victims. In Bodo League, 110,000 Communists and noncombatant sympathizers were massacred by the capitalist regime of the good Christian Syngman Rhee, a friend of General Douglas MacArthur, accused of genocide. At the time, the massacre was attributed to the North Korean Communists, and when the names of the perpetrators and the number of victims were revealed, they were immediately forgotten. Even greater were the executions of leftists in Indonesia in 1966 carried out by Suharto with the support of the CIA: between 500,000 and 1,000,000 were executed.

The same racist practices had been exercised by Washington in the Philippines during the first half of the 20th century. From 1898 to 1946, a long list of massacres of the native population added up to nearly a million dead, almost all civilians, and the invention of new torture methods such as "waterboarding" (*waterboard*), which later became a specialty of the house in several of the far-right military dictatorships in Latin America, all supported by Washington, and more recently in Guantánamo, a lawless province where human rights are violated in Cuba.

As evidence of the repeated and brutal racism suffered by the Philippines, as by so many other territories with "peaceful blacks," browns, and yellows, any of the hundreds of letters sent by American combatants to their families would suffice. For example, on July 20, 1899, the soldier and correspondent for the *New York Evening Post* in the Philippines, H. L. Wells, wrote that "so far no one has questioned the fact that our soldiers in the Philippines shoot blacks for sport... But the American people can be assured that there have been no more Filipino deaths than necessary; at least not more than the British considered necessary to kill in India and Sudan; no more than the French killed in Annam [Vietnam]." Wells was absolutely right. In the early years of the occupation, the United States only killed a few tens of thousands of insignificant Filipinos, no more than France and the United Kingdom. It would continue killing in the following years until reaching the figure of half a million.

Few, like David Thoreau half a century earlier against the war in Mexico, dared to publicly denounce this immorality that victimized the aggressor under the verses of Rudyard Kipling in honor to the altruistic sacrifice of the white race. In 1906, Twain, one of the founders of the New York Anti-Imperialist League and a staunch critic of his own country's atrocities, published an essay analyzing the glory of what the reports hailed as a heroic victory. Under the title "The Moro Massacre," Twain reflected on the "dead or alive" order to solve the problem of a village of a thousand "dark-skinned savages" who had taken refuge in the crater of a mountain, seven hundred meters high. According to the triumphant reports, the villagers couldn't be brought out alive, but they were brought out dead, after a day and a half of shooting from above with state-of-the-art weapons to counter the primitive stones hurled by the besieged from below. With bitter irony, Twain left us a reflective testimony on the true meaning of the words "heroism" and "courage of our troops," who, on March 7, 1906, posed for a photograph in front of a pile of corpses as hunting trophies. "How is it that they call that a battle?... Having completed our four-day siege with the massacre of all those defenseless people."

The fact that the wounded were executed on the ground or that the ammunition used were *dum-dum bullets*, which expand upon entering the victim's body, was also not discussed for long, but some American critics and analysts were struck by the fact that in the war against the Philippines, tens of thousands of deaths were counted with almost no wounded or prisoners, when the historical pattern of wars is the opposite. In the U.S. Civil War, there was one death for every five wounded; in the Philippines, fifteen deaths were reported per wounded. The de facto governor, General Arthur MacArthur, explained this strange statistical phenomenon: "What happens is that men of Anglo-Saxon blood do not die so easily after being wounded as those who belong to inferior races." Little or nothing had changed since the previous century. Little or nothing would change in the century to come.

The same story, the same racism, and the same greed would continue to be expressed through the power of weapons. Seventy years after the first massacres in the Philippines, in the documentary *Hearts and Minds*, U.S. General William Childs Westmoreland, a hero of the Vietnam War and with so many medals they didn't fit on his uniform, declared that "Asians do not understand the value of life. Over there, life is cheap, it's part of their Eastern philosophy, besides, there are so many of them." After World War II against the Nazis, it had become bad taste to speak of race, so the word was replaced with philosophy, ideology, communism, and finally, culture.

The largest number added to the "94 million victims of communism" according to Stéphane Courtois refers to the catastrophic famine in Mao's China in 1958-1962. This famine did not kill 60 million but, most likely and based on various estimates, between 30 and 40 million. In no case was it a deliberate, racist extermination plan, like the Nazi style in Germany, the French in Africa, the British in India, the Americans in Asia and Latin America, or the Japanese in China. This also does not mean that the Chinese are free from racism.

One of the most recognized researchers in the Western press on this topic, Chinese historian and dissident Yang Jisheng, in his book Tombstone (Hong Kong, 2012), estimated a figure of 36 million, though he later considered "40 million who could have been born." He is not referring to unborn fetuses (a simple mathematical calculation) but to those millions who would have been conceived if their parents had not died years earlier. If we apply this same criterion to the tragedies caused by capitalism, the numbers would escape the imagination, so I believe it would be better to consider only the direct and indirect victims of each tragedy; not the hypothetical ones or those whose lives never began.

On the other hand, the texts that denounce these deaths by starvation in China as proof of communist brutality present the tragedy as if the famine were a unique and singular event, without considering that hunger and death in the Asian giant were the norm. Even the famines, which became more frequent and deadly after capitalist companies and their armed extensions of European powers decided to harass, blockade, and vampirize China through their commercial fleets since the 16th century, turning the world's largest economic power into a sea of misery, especially from the Opium War of 1839-42 until the Japanese occupation of 1937, which also left millions dead. From 1810 to 1849, various famines killed 45 million Chinese people. Although historians attribute much of this tragedy to droughts, following the same analytical criteria applied to the 1958 famine, one might also consider the responsibility of the government, then under the dictatorship of Western companies and the British navy. The same can be said of the famine that in 1907-1911 killed 25 million Chinese (according to experts, it was actually worse than the 1958-62 famine) due to three months of rain, lack of civil infrastructure, lack of social plans to address it, and the repression by government forces of the rebellions stemming from the catastrophe.

The need for industrialization in the Soviet Union first and in China later was repeated in younger and less populated countries like Brazil and Argentina, and their only sin was having arrived late and, in China's case, having combined disastrous policies (essentially disruptive of traditional production practices) with climatic problems. Despite everything, life expectancy in China began to improve rapidly from the 1960s onward. From 1960 until Mao's death in 1976, it rose from 44 years to 65. That is, an increase of 21 years, while during the same period, the gain in the United States, during its decade of greatest economic power, was only two years (from 70 to 72).

We will not consider here the case of the Great Depression in the United States in the 1930s, as there is an academic gap on this topic. The one million Mexicans sent into exile (including 60 percent U.S. citizens with Mexican faces) and the deaths due to massive famine are often dismissed with arguments like: during the Great Depression, life expectancy did not decrease but rather increased, as there were fewer traffic accidents and fewer people smoked and drank alcohol (even though these last two factors never have an immediate effect but rather manifest over many years). This is a topic for another chapter and for further years of research.

Let's return to tragedies better analyzed by experts. In India, the reality was no better than in Mao's China, but rather the opposite, yet it did not face the powerful attack of Western propaganda machinery. Starting in 1950, the new democratic state of India improved the life expectancy of its population, but this was not due to any plan; it was simply the result of no longer being a starving, brutalized, and exploited colony of the British Empire, which between 1880 and 1920 alone was directly responsible for the death of 160 million people. Nevertheless, during this period of capitalist democracy in India, deaths attributable to the absence of social reforms continued to pile up—at least 100 million. The globally acclaimed economist and Harvard University professor Amartya Sen and Jean Drèze of the London School of Economics, in 1991, published *Hunger and Public Action*, where they rigorously analyzed several forgotten cases of global famines caused by systems, models, and political decisions. In Chapter 11, they observed: "Comparing India's mortality rate of 12 per thousand with China's rate of 7 per thousand and applying that difference to a population of 781 million in India in 1986, we arrive at an estimate of the excess normal mortality in India of 3.9 million per year. That is, every eight years more people died in India due to a higher regular mortality rate than those who died in China during the gigantic famine of 1958-1961. India has filled its closet with more skeletons every eight years than China put there during its years of shame." The major press did not take note, and the world remained unaware. On the contrary, six years later, as if by magic, *Le Livre noir du communisme* and others of the same commercial genre selling fast and being quickly consumed surfaced.

The Chinese famine of 1958-1962 was one of the worst in history, but not the only or the largest, primarily because of China's population scale. But the government at the time was not the only one to blame nature for its serious administrative errors. A similar story unfolded with the famine in Ireland in 1847-1852. If China lost three percent of its population, Ireland lost 12 percent, and it was not due to communism but rather to the most pure and rapacious capitalism. The tragedy in Ireland was a consequence of London's policies and the dominant ideology. The tragedy translated into a positive impact in the United States with millions of new young workers, just where the ideas that had created the catastrophe in Ireland and other regions of the planet were beginning to proliferate.

If we use the same criteria as the highly publicized book by Courtois to count the dead—from famines caused by systems and government administration to direct massacres—communism cannot possibly compete with the death toll of capitalism. It would suffice to count the millions of indigenous people killed in the three Americas (excluding the initial millions due to unintentional diseases and including exploitation), massacres, dispossession, famines caused by displacement, racism, and negligence. We would then have to add the 15 million Africans who died in North America alone, human beings traded and cataloged as "private property" by the culture and laws of the time. Enslaved individuals who, in the United States, once emancipated by law, received no compensation but were instead thrown into urban poverty. Every time there were economic compensations, they went to white masters for the loss of their private property. Or compensation had to be paid to the imperial powers, as was the case with Haiti, which, between 1826 and 1947, had to pay France compensation of 21 billion dollars (in today's value) for damages. That is, for having taken land and enslaved people from the masters of the French Empire. All with the support of Washington, which did not want a republic of Black people in 1804, just as it would not want another in Cuba in 1898, a few miles closer.

We previously mentioned the 45 million deaths in the Chinese famine of the 19th century, but there were many others in other countries, worse than the Chinese famine of 1958-1962. In Asia, for example, we can consider the Indian famine of 1770, in which over 30 million people died, a direct consequence of the "laws of the free market" imposed by London by force of cannon and administered by the mega-private company East India Company. In 1876, El Niño caused a drought in India. This climatic phenomenon was known to the population, which had adapted to periodic droughts, avoiding famines that would follow the period administered by Britain. The enclosure and privatization of land and rivers deprived millions of people of emergency access to communal resources such as firewood, fodder for livestock (which, in turn, produced fertilizer for plantations), and crucial access to irrigation water. Within a few years, ten million Indians died as a result of the capitalist model for the success of nations. The same phenomenon repeated in 1896 and 1902 with even more devastating consequences: another 20 million people died of hunger, even though the country had a surplus of grains and other food. What happened? The same as always: the food reserves were sent to London and the rest of the developed continent, as scarcity due to the climatic phenomenon had driven up food prices on European markets.

Between 1880 and 1920, 165 million Indians died due to the administrative brutality of the British Empire. Later, Winston Churchill admitted: "I hate Indians. They are a beastly people with a beastly religion." In the early 1930s, like many among the wealthiest class in the United States, Churchill admired Adolf Hitler and Benito Mussolini—and acted according to his convictions. In 1943, he took agricultural production from Bengal to feed his army in Somalia, devastating its fragile economy. The mountain of starvation deaths in that year alone exceeded three million. All based on the same criteria applied to Ireland a century earlier: first Britain, then the inferior races. Amid rivers of corpses, 19th-century London administrators explained the Irish tragedy: the Irish were an inferior race and had to learn the rules of the market. The same story a century later, while fighting Nazi racism in Europe (they were actually fighting for their own interests): the Bengalis, like the Irish a century earlier, were an inferior race and had to learn the rules of the free market. Racism and self-interest. Neither market nor free market. What matters first is our development and well-being, and second, that history and people will repeat what the winners say. Therefore, more important than the truth is winning.

Courtois's book also lists two million deaths in North Korea attributed to communism out of a total of three million deaths, without considering that the indiscriminate bombings by General Douglas MacArthur and other "defenders of freedom" wiped out 80 percent of the country. Starting in 1950, hundreds of tons of bombs were often dropped in a single day, all of which, according to Courtois and his Miami repeaters, were not responsible for the deaths of many people. The same method applied in Japan a few years earlier, under the conviction that killing Japanese caused no remorse. That is, the perfect continuation of the racist mentality of the slave-owning South, a combination of disdain for inferior beings and the abuse of the only solution at hand: firearms, bombs from the sky as a divine solution.

In Japan, General LeMay had been the mastermind who planned the bombing of several cities, such as Nagoya, Osaka, Yokohama, and Kobe, between February and May 1945, three months before the atomic bombs of Hiroshima and Nagasaki. On the night of March 10, LeMay ordered the dropping of 1,500 tons of explosives on Tokyo from 300 B-29 bombers. 500,000 bombs rained down from 1:30 AM to 3:00 AM. 100,000 men, women, and children died in just a few hours, and one million others were seriously injured. A precursor to Napalm bombs, these fire gels stuck to houses and human flesh were successfully tested. "Women ran with their babies like torches of fire on their backs," recalled Nihei, a survivor. "I'm not bothered about killing Japanese," General LeMay had said, the same man who less than two decades later would recommend to President Kennedy dropping a few atomic bombs on Havana as a way to solve the problem of the bearded rebels. In the early 1980s, Secretary of State Alexander Haig would tell President Ronald Reagan: "Just give me the order and I'll turn that shitty island into an empty parking lot."

Courtois also counts one million deaths in Vietnam due to the communists, without considering that it was a war of independence against the imperial powers of France and the United States, which left at least two million dead, most not in combat but under the classic American aerial bombardment inaugurated in 1927 against Sandino in Nicaragua and the use of the chemical Agent Orange, which not only wiped a million innocent people off the map indiscriminately but whose effects on genetic mutations are still felt today. With absolute frivolity, he mentions the use of "Yellow Rain," based on an accusation by Reagan's Secretary of State Alexander Haig about poisoning by the Soviet Union in Vietnam, Laos, and Cambodia in 1977. This accusation was proven baseless by a field study by Harvard professor Matthew Meselson, who concluded that the levels of trichothecene mycotoxins occur naturally in the region's vegetation. The genocide perpetrated by Washington with Agent Orange was not only proven, but thousands of U.S. soldiers sued their government for being affected by the chemical. The Vietnamese were still something similar.

He also attributes the barbarity of the Khmer Rouge regime in Cambodia entirely to "communism," solely because the regime was communist, without mentioning that Pol Pot had been supported by Washington and Western corporations; that it was communist Vietnam, which defeated the United States, that put an end to that barbarity while the West continued to support the genociders by recognizing them at the UN as the legitimate government until the 1980s. Between 1969 and 1973, more bombs (500,000 tons) fell on Cambodia than on Germany and Japan during World War II. The same happened to North Korea and Laos. In 1972, President Nixon asked: "How many did we kill in Laos?" To which his Secretary of State, Ron Ziegler, replied: "About ten thousand, maybe fifteen thousand." Henry Kissinger added: "In Laos, we also killed about ten thousand, maybe fifteen thousand." The communist dictator who would follow, Pol Pot, would far surpass that number, massacring one million of his own people. The Khmer Rouge, children of the anti-colonialist reaction of the West, were supported by China and the United States. Another communist regime, the Vietnam that defeated the United States, put an end to Pol Pot's massacre after the slaughter of 30,000 Vietnamese. Apart from those massacred by Washington's bombs in Laos and Cambodia alone, tens of thousands more continued to die after the war ended, due to bombs that did not explode when dropped.

We could go on recalling the direct complicity with Hitler's massacres, before and during World War II, of the most powerful companies, paradigms of capitalist success, such as the Associated Press news agency, JPMorgan (Chase Bank), Ford, GM, Texaco, Alcoa, and dozens of other famous firms that still operate successfully today. For example, IBM, a company that provided services to Hitler from 1933 for the massive data processing that allowed the location of Jews and Gypsies, who would later be exterminated.

We could continue this obscene tally of massacres perpetrated by the ideology that is considered the paradigm of freedom and human rights—coups d'état and military dictatorships orchestrated and supported by the invisible hand of capitalism, secret agencies, and the more visible hands of Washington, London, Paris, Brussels, and the powerful corporations of the developed world.

To consider just a few illustrative examples, let's recall the military coup planned and executed by the CIA in Guatemala in 1954, based on fake news, which not only destroyed the nascent democracy in that country (accustomed to being ruled by brutal dictatorships serving the United Fruit Co.) but also left 200,000 dead over four decades of systematic massacres of Indigenous people and poor peasants—a so-called "civil war" in the press. By the mid-1960s, in Indonesia, nearly a million suspected leftists were executed by the regime of General Suharto, imposed and sustained by the CIA, as a way to rid itself of Sukarno, the revolutionary founder of independent Indonesia and one of the founders of the Non-Aligned Movement, which sought to remain outside the disputes between Washington and Moscow. For a time, media propaganda convinced national and international audiences that the killings had been carried out by a communist group attempting to overthrow Sukarno. History turned out to be the opposite, and it was accepted as encyclopedic fact when the truth was no longer dangerous: it was a CIA and London plot to eliminate Indonesia's independence and development efforts and open it up to the "free market."

There can be no independence for weaker countries without political and cultural unity, something modern empires understood from the very first day and their servants, the local oligarchies, insist on sabotaging. Colonialism was replaced by brutal puppet rulers beholden to developed countries. Almost at the same time as CIA mercenaries were massacring in Indonesia, in Ghana, the revolutionary independence leader and also the first president of the new country, Kwame Nkrumah, was ousted by another tragic coup d'état in 1966. Nkrumah was in favor of the Pan-African League. Like Sukarno, like Patrice Lumumba in Congo, like Thomas Sankara in Burkina Faso in the 1980s, Nkrumah suffered firsthand for his audacity in demanding dignity and attempting to secure independence for his people.

In November 1986, French President François Mitterrand visited Burkina Faso. Its leader, Thomas Sankara, received him without deference and reproached him for
supporting the racist regime in South Africa. At the time,
Mandela remained imprisoned and was on Washington and
London's terrorist list. Thirty years earlier, in 1957, then-
Minister of Justice François Mitterrand had acknowledged:
"Without Africa, France will have no history in the 21st century." A youthful sin. Almost a year after the truths Mitterrand had to hear from Sankara in Burkina Faso and just days
after participating in a commemoration of the twentieth anniversary of Che's assassination in Bolivia, "The African Che"
was killed in a coup d'état. Sankara also (or especially) had
committed the sin of rejecting any monetary assistance from
the World Bank and IMF and, worse still, he hadn't fared
poorly at all. Quite the opposite. His economic, social, and
ecological plans were an overwhelming success, never
acknowledged by the global media. After his assassination
and the coup d'etat, international banks like the IMF and the
ever-thirsty corporations returned like vultures to a country
on its knees, continuing to sow dependency and exploitation
in the name of freedom and the free market. Not only were
social advancements erased in one fell swoop; the economy
also collapsed. After sustained growth since Sankara began
his presidency, the population's per capita income would
take more than a decade to return to the levels reached at the
time of the coup.

More recently, Libya's Muammar Gaddafi proposed reviving Nkrumah's idea of an African Union and was also overthrown and killed in 2011, in the name of freedom, as if it had all been a spontaneous rebellion of the people against a dictator—and with the same tragic consequences as always.

The imperial psychopathology did not end with the traditional colonies. Neither did the psychopaths, in the strict psychiatric sense of the word. Then-Secretary of State under President Obama, Hillary Clinton, summed up the outcome in a televised interview with a reference to Julius Caesar and a self-satisfied laugh that speaks volumes of academic analysis: "*We came, we saw, he died.*" Currently, Libya's per capita income is half of what it was fifteen years ago, not to mention the social chaos, the resulting deaths, and the cardboard-cutout freedom and independence imposed once again by capitalism and its fictional discourse of freedom and free markets.

We could continue with multiple other dictatorships in Africa and Latin America, with general-led mafias like Operation Condor in South America, which pursued, tortured, and assassinated tens of thousands of dissidents with Washington's support and blessing. We could continue with brutal economic blockades on non-aligned countries like Cuba, Iraq, Iran, and Venezuela. Or with the systematic hijacking of new technologies, with deaths caused by pollution from companies like Phillip Morris, Monsanto, Pepsi, Nestlé, or the persistent destruction of the planet based on consumption, pollution, deregulation, and the stripping of governmental and popular power in rational sustainability policies that might contradict the ideology of corporate profits at any cost.

To conclude this brief summary, let's return to capitalist colonies outside Europe. In the chapter "Freedom for the Elite," we analyze the position of Indian-British intellectual and diplomat Shashi Tharoor and professors Jason Hickel and Dylan Sullivan on the impact of imperial policies of capitalism, which contradicts the most promoted popular narratives by mainstream media and government agencies, which could be summarized in one of their conclusions: "In all regions studied, integration into the capitalist world system was associated with wages falling below the subsistence minimum, a deterioration in human stature, and a resurgence in premature mortality."

If, with the same criteria as Courtois and his echo chambers, we continued to count the millions of Indigenous people killed in the Americas during the process that made capitalism possible in Europe, the at least ten million dead (half the population, aside from the other half mutilated or traumatized) that Belgian King Leopold II left in the enterprise called Congo, dedicated to the extermination of elephants for their ivory, rubber for the booming automotive industry, copper, and everything else that the so-called uncivilized savages could extract from their own country, and so many other massacres of Blacks in Africa that don't matter, or in India, or in Bangladesh, or in the Middle East, we could easily reach several hundred million dead in any Black Book of capitalism.

More than that. Renowned economist and professor at Jawaharlal Nehru University, Utsa Patnaik, has calculated that Britain stole 45 trillion dollars from India between 1765 and 1938 alone and caused, over those centuries, the deaths not of a hundred million but of more than a billion people. The figure reached in her book published by Columbia University Press in New York, while it may seem exaggerated at first glance, is no less exaggerated than the one attributed by Courtois based on the same criteria—only it is better documented.

Only one narrative captures the headlines and millions of little tweets and other opinions. That is, they reach their goal: in hijacked democracies, it doesn't matter the weight of truth but the sum of opinions.

The fanaticism of guns and foundational racism

The sacred verse of conservatives in the United States is the Second Amendment approved in 1789. Like any verse from any sacred book, it is brief and open to different interpretations. As in any religion, these are theological interpretations, meaning political ones.

A truly conservative interpretation leads us to conclusions few conservatives desire. Thomas Jefferson (his books were banned for atheism) held the undogmatic view that all laws should be changed according to each generation's needs. But both Jefferson and the rest of the "founding fathers" were racists, a detail not acknowledged even by today's racists.

The amendment's verse reads:

> *"A well-regulated Militia, being necessary to the security of a free State, the right of the people to keep and bear Arms, shall not be infringed"* (Being necessary to the security of a free State, the right of the people to keep and bear Arms shall not be infringed.)

Five words are key to understanding what the amendment means:

1. *militia,* 2., 3. *free State,* 4. *people, and* 5. *Arms.*

Let's start with the last one.

5. *Arms.* Just as the word "car" meant something quite different in the 17th century than what it means today—hence the new traffic laws—the same applies to the word "*arms,*" which referred to a *flintlock* or a *musket.* In any case, for someone to kill another person, they had to be within a few meters and, after firing, had to perform a manual task to reload. For several decades now, people and judges have understood that with the word "arms" in 1789, the (sacred) founding fathers also meant an AR-15 and other assault rifles capable of killing, from a much greater distance, dozens of people before anyone can manage to run or defend themselves.

4. *People.* From the Constitution of 1787 itself, the word "*people*" in "*We the people*" meant "white, slave-owning men." By no means did it include Black people, Indigenous people, or poor whites. But a word is an *ideolexicon*, that is, a bag for carrying different goods.

3., 2. *Free State.* The idea of "*free states*" opposed to "slave states" belongs to the advanced 19th century, which debated abolishing slavery, long after expanding it into Indigenous and Mexican territories where slavery either did not exist or was illegal. In 1789 and for several generations after, the "free state" was the white slave state. Indeed, in all letters, congressional transcripts, and newspaper articles, it is taken for granted that the "free race" was the white race, as others were incapable of understanding freedom. Slavery expanded in the name of Law, Order, and Liberty. The third stanza of the national anthem, written in 1814 by Francis Scott Key, proclaims:

> "*No refuge could save the hireling and slave*
> *From the terror of flight, or the gloom of the grave.*"

The song by this lawyer was motivated by the British burning of the government house in Washington, later painted white by slaves to hide the memory of the fire. England sought to punish a similar attack by the Americans on Canada, when they desired that territory as the fourteenth state. Many enslaved Blacks sided with the invader, for obvious reasons, and the patriot Scott Key, a lawful slaveholder, poured his poetic wrath into the famous song, now the national anthem.

1. Militia. As anyone in their right mind can realize, the expression "a well-regulated Militia" does not mean individuals acting on their own. But that is not all. Both in the 17th and 19th centuries, these militias were the police of the slave-holders. How could a handful of white masters subjugate a majority of Black slaves? Not by the whip but by firearms. But because the masters formed alliances within each state and across slave states, armed militias were of vital importance to safeguard the lives of the white masters and the system itself, which produced the richest men in the country, enslaved 19th-century capitalism, even as the North was already an old hub of commercial and industrial development.

Every right is regulated, and every interpretation depends on the political interests of the moment. Let's look at a radical and absurd example related to the First Amendment, to which I count myself as a staunch defender.

In 2010, the Supreme Court (with a strong majority of judges appointed by conservative presidents) ruled in favor of Citizens United, a "nonprofit" organization advocating for the rights of large corporations. Its founder, Floyd Brown, defined it this way: "We're people who don't care about politics; people who want the government to leave us alone; but if our country calls us to fight abroad, we'll gladly do so." To this old Anglo-Saxon fanaticism, the brutal interventions in other countries are not political or about economic interests but pure patriotism, God, and morality.

In the lawsuit and the final ruling, five out of nine members of the Supreme Court understood that limiting donations from any group to a candidate constituted a "violation of freedom of expression." Moreover, they gained the right to do so anonymously, which academics refer to as "dark money." Of course, once again, in "The Land of Laws," everything is made legal. Corruption is something for Latin Americans and poor Blacks in Africa.

As often happens in a democracy like that of the United States, hijacked by corporations, the citizens had a different opinion. At the beginning of 2010, a poll by ABC and The Washington Post revealed that 80 percent of Americans opposed the removal of restrictions and limits on political donations proposed by Citizens United.

The (political) interpretations against regulations always favor those in power. No one claims that every airport in the United States violates the Constitution because carrying weapons is not allowed. The age to freely purchase assault rifles is 18, but if it were up to gun fanatics, it would be six years old, when the victim enters a school and does not feel free and safe. But the limit of 18 years is still a regulation. Where does it say that in the Second Amendment?

Meanwhile, 40,000 people die each year in this country from gun violence. It's no coincidence that massacres often have a racial motivation against "the inferior races," as that obsession is in the DNA of this country's history. Blacks, Asians, or "Hispanics" do not massacre whites out of hatred. The problem of crime in Black neighborhoods stems from this same history of discrimination: when they became citizens, they were immediately segregated at gunpoint through various policies such as the construction of highways or the criminalization of certain drugs introduced into the country by the CIA itself and used by Nixon, deliberately, to criminalize Blacks and Latinos.

This is the concept of freedom of those who suffer from a paranoia that doesn't let them be free. And they impose it on others in the name of freedom—as in the times of legal slavery, defended even by the "happy slaves."

Prohibiting ideas in the name of freedom of expression

In 2021, Florida Governor Ron DeSantis, in tune with the neofascist president of Brazil, Captain Jair Bolsonaro, signed a law allowing university students to record professors to detect any ideological tendencies. Provided it wasn't the "true" ideology. In December of that year, the governor signed another bill to "give businesses, employees, children, and families the tools necessary to fight against the indoctrination called WOKE" ("awake" in African American dialect), which proposes a re-reading of history from the perspective of groups marginalized by power. For the fanatics, taking a five-year-old child to a religious temple every week or planting them in front of the television for four hours a day to consume mercantilist propaganda isn't indoctrination. But if a

20-year-old enters a university where they might learn some new idea, then that is "indoctrination" and "brainwashing."

The law prohibiting open discussion on racism (the time will come to ban the word *imperialism*) because young white students might feel uncomfortable studying slavery and discrimination, was coupled with another law from the same office, which bans public secondary schools from speaking about the existence of gays and lesbians in the name of fighting "against gender ideology." The dominant gender ideology for centuries, machismo, is not up for discussion. On the contrary, it must be protected through fanatical ignorance.

A specialty of the champions of freedom is to prohibit everything that doesn't align with their interests, like the *Individual Freedom Law* that prohibits any company from requiring its employees to take anti-racism awareness courses. Their repeated "freedom of expression" is freedom for harassment and censorship. This tsunami of prohibitions in education and academia is only the continuation of the ban on dozens of books initiated earlier in the United States, in the best banana republic style. This same ideology, with its phrases and tics copied from American libertarians, is repeated like a copy-and-paste in Latin America, echoing the articles and doctrines planted by the CIA in dozens of countries, which germinated, matured, and continue to bear fruit decades after the Cold War.

Sooner or later, they were going to come for the universities. It is the biggest thorn in the side of the Successful

Businessmen and their butlers. Culture and universities have not been easy to buy, although corporations have done a good job commercializing education and research. According to conservative fanatics, universities are bastions of liberals (leftists) where young people are indoctrinated. They complain that most professors are left-leaning and that, therefore, legislation must be enacted to balance the proportion of conservatives. No similar proposal exists to balance ideologies in powerful churches, multimillion-dollar corporations, stock exchanges, powerful Washington lobbies, or unlimited donations to political parties.

The natural solution to balance political tendencies in universities is for the Future Businessmen to finally get serious about studying for once in their damn lives. But of course, if someone loves money and power, they will hardly invest decades doing research for free. Especially knowing that, after decades of others' efforts, when the results appear, the Successful Businessmen will immediately hijack them in the name of Freedom.

In theory, fascism and liberalism are opposites. Yet, decades ago, neoliberalism (economic) managed to combine a diverse menu into one package. Thus, within the same party were the most radical capitalists and warmongers alongside Christians who had nothing to do with the Jesus of the Gospels, but rather with Judas, someone who could sell his own friend for thirty pieces of silver. Thus, defending Jesus came to mean defending the merchants unjustly expelled from the temple and shoving the damned camel through the eye of the damned needle, while also supporting the empires that crucified other rebels. The lords of money, the corporate boards that spread banana republic dictatorships around the world and legalized dictatorships within their own countries, all in the name of freedom and democracy, as in the times of slavery, managed to unite the two opposing ideologies. The neoliberals of the latter half of the 20th century are today's libertarians, and they drink at the bar with neo-Nazis and neo-fascists with absolute comfort.

Of course, not all are fans of the Holy Office. In August 2022, federal judge Mark Walker temporarily blocked Florida's "Anti WOKE" law, arguing that, according to the law, "professors may exercise their 'academic freedom' as long as they express only those points of view that the State approves." Logical, but temporary. A month later, Governor DeSantis swept the elections. He was re-elected as governor and positioned himself as one of the strongest Republican candidates for the 2024 presidential race.

Every time a conservative politician stokes the anger of the Inquisition, they achieve excellent results. Which proves, once again, that we continue marching toward a new Middle Ages. All with the silence, timidity, or complicity of academia and what was once the heroic resistance for Civil Rights.

While some academics are too preoccupied with a model that explains inflation in the Maldives or how to cite Socrates in a journal no one will read, the Businessmen continue with their plans to neutralize or take possession of one of the last corners of society that they still cannot fully dominate, despite the commercialization of education. I've heard that, "well, that's the job of the professors." That is, they shouldn't concern themselves with the big politics. It's not their thing.

No one says the same about a successful casino owner or a pillow salesman who aspires to be governor or president. No, because the Successful Businessmen are used to commanding and being successful... Not a few professors remain silent, fearing what in assemblies and hallways is repeated as "*fear of retaliation*" for saying what they think. Even the "*tenured*" fear protesting, even though legally they are untouchable.

In the United States, *tenure* was created in 1940 to prevent professors from being fired for their radical or inconvenient ideas and opinions. For this same reason, *tenure* has been under attack in this country for years. Not only is there an attempt to eliminate it, but it has been reduced to a minimum, with a dual purpose: (1) to precarize academic work (depress wages) and (2) to silence inconvenient theories for the dominant dogma.

But professors with *tenure* fear other forms of retaliation. For example, the reduction of their salaries, something that authorities later fail to explain without resorting to childish excuses based on the dominant dogma, such as the Law of Supply and Demand... As if that law weren't overloaded with politics.

In this way, we professors are also neutralized in our ethical commitment to the rest of society, transformative knowledge, the challenge of established norms, and the fight for a better society and world.

Gender ideology

In December 2021, conservative activist Lisa Hansen denounced that she had heard that schools were placing sandboxes in bathrooms for "students who identify as cats." The fantasy was repeated by several Republican politicians throughout 2022, such as Minnesota Senator Scott Jensen, Tennessee legislators, Heidi Ganahl from Colorado, Republican nominee Catalina Lauf from Illinois, at least 20 other candidates for representatives, and multiple parents in school assemblies across the United States, all outraged by "gender ideology." The denunciations went viral, reaching millions of views on some TikTok videos. No sandbox was ever found in any school, nor any group claiming to identify as cats. The most obvious—the hatred of people different from us but with the same rights—passed in front of everyone, like invisible air.

Not coincidentally, and simultaneously, in the parliaments of Latin America, representatives of the right expressed similar indignations, though they did not go as far as the fantasy of the cats.

European royalty wore wigs, stockings, and high heels (a sign of masculinity, since Muslims invented them for faster riding; with that and their own fanaticism, they conquered an empire). A few generations ago, upper-class boys were dressed as girls for photos (see President F. D. Roosevelt, as a child, for example). Everyone dressed in white. Pink and light blue as gendered colors did not exist until the 20th century, an invention of major U.S. stores for commercial reasons: at first, pink was masculine and light blue feminine, but by a fortuitous twist, pink was assigned to girls and light blue to boys, and fanatics said it had been that way since the creation of the world.

None of this is *natural* but cultural products that uneducated people do not understand, and for that very reason, they get offended and deliver speeches full of convictions in parliaments and from their virtual platforms.

"Gender ideology" is not a recent evil that will destroy humanity, but as old as the first religions: it is machismo, with its need for power and sexual fears.

Neomedievalism. The problem is others' freedom

Let's begin by repeating something as old as the internet: the definition of "pro-life" is not only deeply hypocritical but assumes that pro-abortion movements are "anti-life." Not even those who define themselves as "pro-abortion" consider abortion a good or fun thing but, in special circumstances, a lesser evil, the result of structural, social, cultural, and individual problems.

In this sense, we can say that the recent decision by the U.S. Supreme Court against the right to abortion under special circumstances (leave to the discretion of the states) is just another stop on the road back to the Middle Ages. It is not merely a cultural change (most likely a reaction to a larger progressive historical movement toward the expansion of "equal freedom") but, as always, part of a strategy that protects the economic micro-minorities, who at some point will become the center of conflicts and demands of the new generations. They know this and need to distract from the problem by creating political combos where their political-economic programs are aligned with a popular god or some private moral fanaticism deeply rooted in society. In the Anglo-Saxon, Protestant world, this element must have something sexual and puritanical about it. The warlike crusades that leave millions dead in the name of Christian love are fine.

Last year, Florida Governor Ron DeSantis , the leading contender for the White House in 2024, made headlines with the decision to ban history and math books that referred to Critical Race Theory and any other questioning or revelation about the endemic racism of his country in primary and secondary schools. In the same way, he managed to pass the law known as "Don't Say Gay , according to which the youth of this country can talk about wars, drugs, and rapes, but not about the mere existence of people who are a little different from us. Since those "different" folks don't interfere in our private lives, we interfere and legislate over theirs, turning them into taboos that not only destroy the psychology of young gay, lesbian , and transgender people but also place our heterosexual children back into the damn repressive and feared cage of toxic machismo that we ourselves suffered.

In the same vein and direction is the Supreme Court. Although it is never openly acknowledged, the Supreme Court is a highly political body, which is why every time one of its nine members dies or retires, a desperate battle begins in Congress to nominate the new judge based on their ideological orientation and disputes over their sexuality or other distractions. The majority of its members (6 out of 9) were nominated by conservative Republican presidents. Five of them were chosen by Presidents George W. Bush (2) and Donald Trump (3), both of whom reached the White House after losing the popular vote in the general elections and thanks to an electoral system designed to protect the slavist system of the scarcely populated (by whites) but powerful South in the 19th century.

Powerful due to its fanaticism. The same fanaticism that in June 2020 confronted a peaceful protest of black citizens demonstrating against police racism with a militarized police force and, six months later, on January 6, 2021, confronted the white Neo-Confederates—armed to the teeth with firearms, another tradition of the fearful and feared slavist South—with mere sticks. Their goal, as known by the FBI , was to stage a coup d'état by storming the Capitol and preventing the confirmation of the new Democratic president.

This power, based on "special rights" of a group largely composed of self-victimizing Confederate admirers and white supremacists, is the only group that has ever posed a real threat to the existence of the very country they now claim to defend like no one else. The same ones who fill their mouths with patriotism and strategically accuse critics, the essence of any democracy , of being "anti-American."

This special power of a minority that assumes as dogma that it is the majority found itself with a vacancy on the Supreme Court in February 2016, when the liberal (left, in American language) Justice Antonin Scalia died. It was up to Democratic President Barack Obama to nominate a replacement, who, obviously, would be of his political line. The Republicans blocked this nomination for almost a year until the new Republican president, Donald Trump , was in the White House and could nominate the conservative Neil Gorsuch.

The last member appointed to the Supreme Court confirms this reasoning. On September 18, 2020, just over a month before the general elections that Joe Biden would win, the liberal Justice Ruth Ginsburg died. The Republicans managed to nominate and approve their conservative candidate Amy Coney Barrett in record time on October 27, 2020, just days before the elections.

Due to this decision by the Court (a highly political body mostly composed of men), the CDC, a government agency, estimates that Black women will experience a 33 percent increase in pregnancy-related deaths. For thousands of women, pregnancy will mean a death sentence.

What's next on this path toward the Middle Ages? One of the members of the Supreme Court, the ultra-conservative Justice Clarence Thomas, made it clear in writing: "In future cases, we should reconsider all substantive due process precedents of this Court, including Griswold [1965, regarding the use of contraceptives], Lawrence [2003, against the criminalization of homosexuality], and Obergefell [$15, in favor of same-sex marriage]."

In other words, the veteran conservative of the Supreme Court stated that the next steps toward this neo-medievalism will be to ban same-sex marriages, criminalize different sexual orientations, and prohibit the use of contraceptive pills.

If we continue along this line of historical regression, we will find that the next step would be the prohibition of divorce and interracial marriage, which was illegal until the Supreme Court lifted its ban in 1967, when Justice Thomas was 19 years old.

Of course, this goal of the modern-day Torquemada might encounter an obstacle. The Justice, a hero of Protestant conservatives, Catholics, and white supremacists, is a Black man (or "African American," although in practice he is less African American than the white Elon Musk) and is married, for the second time, to the conservative activist Ginni Lamp, a blonde woman, a member of the Tea Party and founder of Liberty Central and Liberty Consulting.

Ahhh… the word *liberty* is so beautiful. As long as it doesn't concern someone else's freedom, of course.

The logic of political combos[2]

José sells Mexican tacos and Argentinian choripanes from a cart on Ocho Street and Azúcar Avenue in Miami. He has two employees. Guadalupe, the cook, works from eight in the morning until seven in the evening, and Ronald, the skinny guy from Caracas, handles deliveries whenever José gets an order on his UberFood app. At first, he got along well with both of them, until he started getting irritated every night when he read Guadalupe and Ronald's posts on Facebook. The only thing the three of them have in common is that none of them go to church on Sundays, but Guadalupe and Ronald had turned out to be lefties, something that didn't seem apparent when they were looking for work. One from Monterrey and the other exiled from the Chavez regime didn't seem like cases worth worrying about. But for some mysterious reason, they were "anti-imperialists, not anti-Americans," as the idiot Ernesto said, and nothing is worse than a kick in the balls or having friends who are so politically clueless. He even felt tempted once to spice up Ernesto's choripán with a few drops of laxative, knowing it wouldn't kill him but would screw with him for a while as a deserved reward for his damn rhetoric that had already infected his employees.

---

[2] Names and other details have been changed for legal reasons.

Ernesto would come back from his little gig at the university and stop by the neighborhood shops, as if to immerse himself in the local vibe before returning to his apartment full of books and useless exams, especially at this point in December.

José didn't know if Ernesto was a customer or an enemy. At least that was his dilemma every Friday when he saw him appear with his nearsighted glasses and, without a word, force him to put away his phone. Ernesto would show up and start talking to Ronald. Apparently, they exchanged jokes with the kid ("che" here, "pana" there), but José knew Ernesto was there to annoy him. That's the fate of some individuals—no one knows why or for what they were born. He, José, gave jobs to the cook and to the *delivery guy*, Ronald, and they didn't even grasp how things worked.

Last Friday, Ernesto showed up with his little brown briefcase full of scraps of paper, that crap from his students who have parents paying thousands of dollars for them to graduate with something while working half or quarter-time and then flaunting their little Bachelor of Science or Master of Arts degrees, Doctor of Philosophy and all that useless crap no one knows what it's for.

"I don't get it either, don José," he told me last week, while picking up his food—, why you defend Jeff Bezos so much.

"Nothing personal," I said. "I defend Elon Musk just as much, Warren Buffett…

"The job creators…

"Yep! Who else, if not them, creates jobs?

"They create jobs and create the wealth of this world," he said, with his usual sarcasm. "The Fathers of Humanity's Progress. I say it not with sarcasm but with capital letters, like a New York Times headline.

"You said it, buddy. That's what all entrepreneurs do. With all due respect, it's what I do myself. If it weren't for this humble business, two workers would be begging on a corner of this very Ocho Street.

And he, being a bastard, dumped on me all that must-he-know-from-his-wrinkly-books-or-from-his-wrinkly-brain nonsense:

"For some mysterious reason, small heroic entrepreneurs like you, don José, consider yourselves members of the same guild as Jeff Bezos, Elon Musk, and Warren Buffett…

"Well, maybe because we have something in common…

"Yes, everything except a hundred trillion dollars and the power to crush other small entrepreneurs like you. I don't know, but maybe one day you'll realize you have more in common with Guadalupe and the kid… (what's his name? Ronald, yes, Ronald) than with the darlings Jeff, Elon, and Warren. Seems to me you wouldn't be able to keep working without the Guadalupes, without the Ronalds, but you could probably keep going, and maybe without suffering as much, if Jeff, Elon, and Warren didn't exist. But I don't blame you for that mistake, which isn't just political, but existential. Have you noticed politics always gets a bad rap? The world's owners have always known how to use *Political Combos*. For example, if you're a religious type, let's say Catholic, Protestant, Pentecostal, or *praise-the-Lord*, you'll end up supporting the entire conservative party agenda, that is, you'll end up supporting, with heroic zeal, not just the ban on abortion but the right to carry an M16 rifle on Ocho Street (in the name of Freedom, obviously), the tax cuts for millionaires and the freedom of big capital which, according to the theology, guarantees the freedom of the beggars. The same happens in those countries down south, way down south. Someone divided the field between city and countryside, between civilization and barbarism, and everyone took sides. Boca and River, Pañarol and Nacional, Flamengo and Corinthians, Colo Colo and Universidad, Michigan and Alabama... So, for example, the field laborers, those who get up at five with a mate and go to bed at seven without a Martini Rossi, took sides with the landowners, all to fight the damned city dwellers who, they say, suck their blood. Long live the Patriotic Party! Long live the Homeland! Long live the Parrot's Foot! But talk about idiots, right? And the powerful landowners, the ranchers who own thousands of hectares, the representatives of the people, dress like gauchos in Brazil, Argentina, and Uruguay, like *huasos* in Chile, and like Indian pongos in Peru or Bolivia, and make the toothless poor believe they're part of the same party. Long live the Patriotic Party! Long live the Homeland! Long live the Parrot's Foot! They spoke more or less the same, dressed more or less the same, especially during national holidays, and, like in the times of slavery, when black slaves defended their masters, the wage slaves defend their bosses and fight at parties and elections for the leader's sash, for the master's color, for the family and tradition of the gaucho. Another perfect combo. Tell me you don't remember that "Long live Dr. Whiskygratis!", the CIA's candidate? Nothing has changed much, don't you think? Those in power know how to do it. Otherwise, they wouldn't be in power, right? And I'm not talking about being president of this or that country, because that's not really being in power.

"I don't know," I said, just to end it. "Anyway, the customer is always right. Here's your choripán. It's a house specialty... Or a cart specialty, whatever you want to call it. *Choriarepa*, I call it. It's Argentinian choripán crossed with Venezuelan arepas, with a few drops of Mexican agave. All dissident condiments, just how you like them...

In the end, I went for the laxative instead of the agave. Worse are the others who, they say, use cancer-causing radiation or frequencies that keep you from sleeping.

The terrorism of the war on terrorism

The U.S. Congress has just approved the construction of a War on Terrorism Memorial to be built not far from the Lincoln Memorial, "to honor those who served in the longest conflict in the Nation's history." It won't be the first, as there's already the *Global War on Terrorism Memorial* in Georgia, so that new generations never forget the sacrifice of the

Nation of Laws that, like Superman, fights "for freedom and justice" worldwide. A narrative for children raised in Disney World and for adults who value faith over reason: the world boils down to the struggle of Good against Evil, and we are the guardians of Good, of Manifest Destiny.

As always, myths are loaded with strategic forgetfulness. It wasn't even the longest conflict, as the war of dispossession—not of the *tribe* but of the Seminole Nation—lasted from 1816 to the mid-19th century. Before becoming the mascot of a football team, the Seminoles were genuine heroes in a real *war of defense* against the dispossession of their territory in Florida and against an immense military power disparity. Like other peoples dispossessed and massacred by Anglo-Saxon fanaticism, they were considered savages (terrorists) who, according to President Andrew "Indian Killer" Jackson's 1832 Union address, "attacked us first without provocation."

On August 31, 2021, President Joe Biden announced the "end of the war on terrorism." (Naturally, as we wrote twenty years ago, the war business will shift to the Far East. There will be a Second Cold War in cyberspace, not without the flames of the first.) Since no U.S. president can speak of love but only of war, good old Biden, in a very Obama-esque style, has warned: "let me make it clear: if you seek to harm the United States... you should know that we will never forgive you. We will not forget. We will hunt you to the ends of the Earth, and you will pay for your offense." A literal copy of the warnings to remember and punish the defenses and offenses of others that fill the annals of history over the past two hundred years.

Only the "War on Terrorism" hides the roots of the problem in the same way as the "War on Drugs," designed, according to its authors, to criminalize Black and Latino people. (Beijing has also used this ideolexicon of "War on Terrorism" to justify the violation of the human rights of the Uighur people.) The name "War on Terrorism" and the obligation to never forget hide a systematic forgetfulness, such as the destruction of democracies in the Middle East (like Iran's in 1953), the destabilization of secular governments (like Afghanistan's in the 1970s), the creation of uncontrolled militias (like the Mujahideen or the Contras in the 1980s), the lost and genocidal wars (like Vietnam in the 1960s or Iraq in the 2000s). Like the most recent indiscriminate bombings in Syria and Iraq, leaked by accident but proven to be a systematic resource. (Then, better to criminalize those who exposed us for killing, as in the case of Julian Assange.) Like the indefinite detention of suspects stemming from the Patriot Act of 2003, which has obscenely extended to poor immigrants. Because the poor are always suspects. Because this is The Land of Laws, as the poor who manage to cross and get papers and paperwork like to repeat.

It is impossible to speak of terrorism in the Middle East without considering the role of the Northwestern empires. It is impossible to speak of the role of empires without corporate interests. As long as these exist, imperialism will exist, and so will the bloody "defensive wars." In 1933, Smedley

Butler, the most decorated general of his generation and hero of the Banana Wars, began to reflect and admitted: "I have been Wall Street's muscle, a gangster for capitalism." In 1961, another general, President Eisenhower, before being accused of being a communist, warned of the interference of the Military-Industrial Complex in government. The latest "War on Terrorism" cost $8,000,000,000,000 (twice the economy of all Latin American countries combined), caused the death of over one million people, and displaced another 38 million. How many terrorist groups are needed to reach any of these figures?

So, then, why is this universal absurdity possible? The unjust death of a U.S. citizen due to racial reasons can mobilize millions of outraged individuals, but when a hidden massacre of fifty children in the Middle East is leaked, it goes unnoticed. It doesn't exist. Isn't imperialism the greatest expression of racism? The shameful prison of Guantánamo, the center for Human Rights violations in Cuba, has survived two decades of empty promises because even psychologists have made fortunes advising torturers. Like the CIA's prison ships, Guantánamo is not U.S. territory but occupied territory, and therefore, its humanitarian laws do not apply. Even hundreds of innocent people tortured for years, many released as dry sponges, will never receive compensation but rather stigmatization from the rest of the world. The same goes for the dozens of secret and illegal prisons that the CIA maintains around the world (black sites) as if they were black holes of all human rights, those parallel governments that

Washington upholds while giving lessons on Human Rights.

Besides its own roots, the "War on Terrorism" has managed to hide the real problems of the present. Countries continue their absurd increase in military spending, increasing poverty and violence in nations. The pandemic has exposed its utter uselessness but, on the other hand, has contained massive social protests in "civilized" countries, a growing danger that had previously led to the militarization of the police. (With the predictable exception of the assault on the U.S. Congress on January 6, 2021, where the police confronted the mob of Confederate flags with batons and words of consolation.)

Do you truly want to serve your country? Then, stop with the patriotic self-indulgence and start telling the truth, especially that truth that the people don't want to hear. That requires more courage than pressing buttons and eliminating dozens of innocents from a distance, as if it were a video game. That's not heroism. It's a major crime. But worse than these soldiers indoctrinated by a trillion-dollar machinery is the silence of the citizens, distracted by passionate debates over flares and slogans.

Finally, Biden added: "The fundamental obligation of a president is to defend and protect the United States, not against the threats of 2001, but against the threats of 2021… Thank you, may God protect our troops."

Mr. President, the solution is quite simple and doesn't require more spending but less: stop believing God has a passport and a flag hanging at the entrance of your home. Stop considering preemptive invasions as acts of defense and start complying with international laws. You will save not only your country and the lives of your soldiers, but millions of other human lives.

Of course, that won't be good business for the Lords of War, but, well, someone always has to lose something.

Bomb, baby, bomb. Russia, Argentina, and Mexico

On February 2, 2023, the Republican representative of Cuban exiles in Miami, María Elvira Salazar, introduced a proposal to condemn "the crimes of socialism". The well-known radio and television network José Martí from Miami (which, since 1983, has produced ideological propaganda in favor of the freedom of capitalism and private enterprise, but with government funds exceeding 30 million dollars annually) headlined: "U.S. House of Representatives approves resolution denouncing the horrors of socialism." Of the horrors of capitalism, which are many times more tragic, not a word.

On February 28, the same congresswoman warned Argentina *"in Spanish, to make it clear"* for exercising its sovereignty with the project of an aircraft factory with assistance from China, *"making a pact with the Devil, which could have consequences of biblical proportions,"* she said.

When seventy years ago the democratic and nationalist president of Argentina J. D. Perón initiated the production of the successful Pulqui I and II aircraft, it caused the same alarm. The Pulqui planes were used by the military (the old armed wing of the Creole oligarchy) to overthrow him in 1955. Later, this national industrialization project was dismantled under pressure from Washington, which promised the subsequent dictatorship cheaper planes. Sixty years later, for the same reasons, from her pulpit in the House of Representatives, Congresswoman Salazar raised two fingers and declared: "There are two worlds, the free world and the world of the enslaved."

The messianic dichotomy assumes that the greatest destroyer of democracies and the greatest promoter of friendly dictatorships of the 20th century, the empire built on slavery, land theft, the imposition of its own will, and wars around the globe is, at the same time, "the Free World."

This sort of imperial arrogance is not new and has been exercised with fanaticism on this side of the Atlantic for over two centuries. But no fanaticism (whether religious or political) is possible without persistent proselytism and propaganda. Since the 19th century and, especially, starting with Edward Bernays and the development of mass media in the 20th century, the creation of public opinion became an industry and a meticulously calculated market. In the 21st century, the century of social networks and artificial intelligence, little or nothing has changed. The censorship of that "Free World" continues to be exercised just as in the "Enslaved World," but with methodological differences and the same objective as always: to keep a micro minority in political and economic power.

This representative of 130,000 Miami residents, on behalf of 320 million Americans, assumes that people forget which governments promoted and financed more dictatorships and more coups d'état against sovereign nations and democracies around the world.

Of course, Mrs. Salazar is not alone. More recently, on March 16, the Republican representative from South Carolina, Lindsey Graham, floated the idea of a Third World War as an option to respond to the offense of a U.S. military drone being shot down in the Black Sea. According to Graham, the United States should not limit itself to funding the new war with a hundred billion dollars (always in the name of "the right to self-defense") but should also shoot down Russian planes in retaliation for the "atrocious attack" against our country, which, in reality, took place in the Black Sea, thousands of miles away and a few from the Russian border, and cost zero American lives. All this under the pretext of "they attacked us first, and we must defend ourselves," a mantra endlessly repeated against the invaded Indians, the dispossessed Mexicans, the nonexistent Spanish attack on the Maine, and so on and so forth.

The same Graham had earlier proposed intervening in Mexico or using military drones "to solve" the problem of drug cartels and drugs. For his part, the representative from Texas, Dan Crenshaw, also requested authorization to use military force in Mexico against drug cartels. As history shows since the Monroe Doctrine of 1823, such authorization is not sought from Mexico, but from Washington.

The same unilateral force, that legacy of the enslaving mindset even after abolition, defined itself as "the free race," the very one that considers itself just, divine, and democratic when it neither asks for nor accepts opinions from inferior races, cultures, and peoples. *The free race* by the force of arms that kept the enslaved here and the "peaceful blacks" in the backyard and the tropics over there, under the law of the revolver and the gunboat.

As always, the bravest and most patriotic in the world are those who know they will never go to any war, but some of their donors will make a lot of money from the old business of death.

The fanaticism of Manifest Destiny does not rest. Its voters, its believers, cannot see that there is a simpler, more logical, and effective solution than continuing the arms business. We wrote about this twenty years ago, but we will insist again. Just consider the capitalist law of supply and demand: eliminate or reduce drug consumption in the United States, and the problem of drug trafficking will diminish to its lowest possible point, inevitably. The issue is that (1) it is necessary to invest in a socialist prevention plan, transferring those millions of dollars from the failed War on Drugs to schools and hospitals; (2) the lucrative business of weapons and the capital transferred from the United States to Mexican cartels would be affected. So, it seems better to continue fighting fire with more gasoline. It seems more convenient to harass Mexico, something that has left good profits since its destruction in another fabricated war in 1836 and 1846 to extend "the blessing of slavery" under false flags... Until they end up forcing Mexico to call in Russian or Chinese missiles, as they did with Cuba in 1961 after the Bay of Pigs invasion. Does it seem unthinkable? Well, you can inflate a balloon for a long time, but not forever.

Of course, there are less dramatic options. It's hard to imagine Donald Trump taking the same positions on international policy that the "bad guys" have held for decades, but on March 17 of this year, a modest miracle occurred when he declared that "there must be a complete commitment to dismantle the entire globalist neoconservative establishment that is perpetually dragging us into endless wars, pretending to fight for freedom and democracy abroad, while turning us into a dictatorship and a third-world country."

Why is he doing this? A reaction to Ron DeSantis? Maybe. But that's another topic that doesn't negate what we understand to be a simple and tragic truth. Only for this, after 250 years, a former U.S. president might have some trouble with the law.

Washington, let's talk about reparations

President Joe Biden has announced his intention to exclude Cuba and Venezuela from the Summit of the Americas scheduled for June 22. The Undersecretary of State, Brian

Nichols, explained that undemocratic countries cannot be invited.

Deciding which countries can attend a regional summit is not considered authoritarian by a country that is historically responsible for thousands of military interventions in the region alone, dozens of dictatorships, coups d'état, the destruction of democracies, and massacres of all kinds and colors from the 19th century until yesterday, under the authoritarian practice of imposing its own laws on other countries and violating all agreements with the inferior races that stopped benefiting it.

Washington and the Corporations it serves have not only been the promoters of bloody capitalist dictatorships in the region since the 19th century but also the primary promoters of the much-mentioned communism and the current social, political, and economic reality of Cuba and Venezuela. Now that the governor of Florida has signed a law to teach about the evils of communism in schools, it would be stimulating if teachers didn't limit themselves to the McDonald's menu.

All those crimes and thefts at gunpoint have gone unpunished without exception. In 2010, the Obama administration apologized for the syphilis experiments in Guatemala, but nothing more than a tear. Impunity, the mother of all corruptions, has been reinforced by a sort of Hiroshima Syndrome, where every year the Japanese apologize to Washington for the atomic bombs they dropped on cities full of innocents.

Much of Latin America has suffered and suffers from Hiroshima Syndrome, where not only are reparations not demanded for two hundred years of crimes against humanity, but the victim feels guilty of a cultural corruption instilled by this very brutality. A few days ago, a woman was welcoming her brother at Miami Airport wrapped in an American flag while shouting in Spanish: "Welcome to the land of freedom!". It's the morality of the slave, where, for centuries, the oppressed strived to be "good blacks," "good Indians," "good Hispanics," "good women," "good poor." In other words, obediently exploited.

All of this falls within the economic interests of an empire ("God placed our resources in other countries"), but the racial factor was fundamental in the fanaticism of the white master and the black slave, the wealthy businessman and the poor worker. Currently, the anti-racism movements in the United States have succumbed to a convenient divorce, where global thought and macro-political sensibility are nullified to make room for the micropolitics of atomized demands. One of these, the heroic and justified struggle against racism, loses perspective when it is forgotten that imperialism is not only a racist exercise but was historically fueled by this moral calamity.

Before the emergence of the excuse of "the fight against communism," the open justification was "to bring order to the black republics," because "black people don't know how to govern themselves" or exploit their own resources. Once the Cold War ended, racism was disguised as a "clash of civilizations" (Samuel Huntington) or financial interventions in regions with "sick cultures," like Latin America, or in lands with terrorists of other religions, as in the Middle East, where, in Iraq alone, they left over a million dead, unnamed and without a well-defined number, as tradition dictates.

This morality of the slave was and remains a common practice. In 2021, for example, the conservative favorite candidate for the California governorship, Larry Elder, claimed that it is reasonable for white people to demand reparations for the abolition of slavery, since black people were their property. "Like it or not, slavery was legal," Elder said. "The abolition of slavery took away white masters' property." Elder is a black lawyer on his mother's, father's, grandparents', and great-grandparents' side. In other words, a descendant of private property. By the same logic, Haiti paid compensation to France for over a century.

The California candidate's proposal was a response to movements demanding compensation for the descendants of slaves. One argument against it is that we do not inherit the sufferings of our ancestors, and each person is responsible for their own destiny. Something very much in line with Protestant ethics and worldview: one saves or damns oneself alone. The Protestant doesn't care if their brother or daughter goes to hell if they deserve Paradise. Who isn't happy in Paradise?

But the past is not only alive in culture. It is alive in our institutions and in how class privileges are organized. It would suffice to mention the electoral system of the United States, a direct inheritance of the slave system, by which rural and white states have more representation than more diverse states with ten times their approval. Through this system, in 2016, Trump became president with almost three million fewer votes than Clinton.

Post-slavery segregation is also alive today, with ghettos of Black, Chinese, and Latino people crammed into major cities as heirs to the freedom won in 1865 but without economic sustenance. Not to mention urban segregation policies through highway layouts or the criminalization of certain drugs, all with the stated intention of keeping certain ethnic groups in a state of servitude and demoralization. Not to mention the fortunes amassed in the past, transmitted to groups and families just as noble titles were passed down in the Middle Ages.

I believe Latin Americans are, at the very least, a few centuries behind in terms of economic reparations for destroyed democracies and imposed dictatorships at gunpoint. From the theft of half of Mexico's territory to reinstall slavery to dictatorships in protectorates, the Banana Wars at the beginning of the 20th century, the multiple massacres of workers, the destruction of democracies with the sole aim of eliminating popular protests and protecting the interests of large companies like UFCo., ITT, Standard Oil Co., PepsiCo, or Anaconda Mining Co., all crimes officially acknowledged by Washington and the CIA, would be more than sufficient arguments to demand reparations.

However, as the logic of banks and investors indicates, reparations are always demanded from the victims. The same could be said of Europe, which, for centuries, enriched itself with hundreds of tons of gold and thousands of tons of silver from Latin America, or by massacring tens of millions of Africans while stealing astronomical fortunes that prove "the right path to success" according to Vargas Llosa.

Washington is in no position to moralize, neither within nor beyond its borders. But its arrogance stems from historical ignorance or, more likely, from its faith in popular amnesia. Of course, since we are here to contribute, we remind them of their long history of massacres and sermons. We remind them that there are quite a few unsettled accounts.

Of course, I can understand that solutions, though possible and just, are "too utopian." That's why I'd like to suggest, as my grandmother used to say in the countryside, "gentlemen, you look prettier when you're quiet."

WAR CALLS AGAIN

New enemy wanted

"The enemy never rests… Your mission is ours". So, on the front page, Lockheed Martin, a private company that sells war weaponry (always referencing the "right to defense" and "national security") advertises in the *New York Times*, just in case there's another buyer besides the government. $50,000,000,000 in search of new enemies. On December 31, 2021, the *Wall Street Journal* published an extensive analysis. The title alone begins with a question and ends with the answer: *"Who Won in Afghanistan? Private Contractors. The U.S. military spent 14 trillion dollars ($14 trillions) over two decades of war; the beneficiaries range from major manufacturers to entrepreneurs."* After the new military fiasco in Afghanistan, and after such a fortune invested by Washington in war companies, the merchants of death, it is urgent to find a new enemy and a new conflict. Before a larger adventure with China, the option is clear: continue violating NATO's non-expansion armament treaties eastward, pressure Russia to react by deploying its army on the border with Ukraine, and then accuse it of attempting to invade the neighboring country. Hasn't this been exactly the history of

treaties signed with Native Americans since the late 18th century? Hasn't this been precisely the order and method of action on the Wild Frontier? Treaties with other nations have served to buy time, to consolidate a (strong, base) position. Once they become an obstacle to new expansion, they are violated by accusing the other party of aggression or non-compliance. On the other hand, President Joe Biden needs to recover his declining popularity. Both the unpopularity of presidents and the massive support they receive after proving their masculinity through international bullying constitute a long-standing pattern. It would suffice to recall the doubts about President William McKinley's sexuality, the call to Washington's imperial masculinity, and finally, McKinley himself sending the Maine to Havana in 1898, with which the yellow press fabricated the "Spanish-American War" to steal Cuba from the rebellious Black fighters who were battling Spain. A lucrative business that, judging by the history of the last two hundred years, will be supported by the majority of the American people or by all the powerful figures on Wall Street, London, and Washington.

When was the war in Ukraine decided?

On November 22, 2021, Washington announced the end of the war in Afghanistan. After twenty years of continuous occupation, hundreds of thousands of deaths, and an increase in opium trafficking; after eleven years since the official death of one of the CIA's creations, Osama bin Laden, Washington withdrew nearly all its operational troops from the country.

The sudden urgency, after a two-decade delay, generated chaos: not only was the country left to the supposed enemies, the Taliban (another offshoot of the mujahideen, terrorists developed by the CIA), but they were also gifted millions of dollars in military equipment, from tanks to all kinds of ammunition.

The chaos and mysterious urgency were visible in the desperation of collaborators and new refugees, a déjà vu of Vietnam, another historical defeat for the world's greatest military power. Images of desperate people trying to scale the walls of Kabul's airport, families handing over their children to the valiant marines to be rescued from evil, are a historical genre of media propaganda that nullifies any critical view of reality. To illustrate this, it would suffice to republish the articles of the anti-imperialist Mark Twain, responding to Rudyard Kipling's poem, "The White Man's Burden," which went viral in 1899 by order of Theodore Roosevelt.

On December 31, the Wall Street Journal asked: "Who won in Afghanistan?" The same article answered: "the private contractors." Washington spent 14 trillion dollars [over seven times the economy of Brazil] during two decades of war. Those who benefited range from major arms manufacturers to entrepreneurs."

Following the significant collapse in Afghanistan, we published something that is becoming increasingly clear: the only thing we could expect is another war. What other reason, if not, could be behind this desperate change in strategy and a clear realignment of forces? Wars are big business for private corporations, but governments must provide tsunamis of money, in addition to planning a defeat that can be sold as a victory—and part of the geopolitical reasons, of course.

On January 24, 2022, a month before the Russian invasion of Ukraine, we insisted in another article ("New Enemy Wanted") that "after the new military fiasco in Afghanistan, and after such a fortune invested by Washington in war companies, merchants of death, it is urgent to find a new enemy and a new conflict. Before a greater adventure with China, the option is clear: continue violating the treaties [the promise] of NATO arms expansion to the East, pressure Russia to react by deploying its army on the border with Ukraine, and then accuse it of trying to invade the neighboring country. Hasn't this been exactly the history of the treaties signed with Native Americans since the late 18th century? Hasn't this been precisely the order and method of action on the Wild Frontier? Treaties with other peoples have served to buy time, to consolidate a (strong, base) position."

Almost a year earlier, in January 2021, the State Department had already threatened European companies with sanctions if their governments continued with the construction of Nord Stream II. "We are informing companies about the risks they face, and we invite them to withdraw from the agreement before it is too late," a government source reported, according to Reuters on January 12. This 11-billion-dollar project would have meant extremely cheap natural gas for Europe, but it was going to harm Ukraine with the loss of royalties from the rights to cross their country with older pipelines.

In September of that year, leaks from Nord Stream II were reported in the Baltic Sea, just after the works were completed. According to Sweden and Denmark, "someone deliberately bombed it," but the major Western press barely covered it and, when it did, labeled it as "a mystery" whose main suspect was Russia, the primary victim. A classic media warfare tactic, which the White House supported. In November, prosecutor Mats Ljungqvist reported the discovery of explosive residues at the site, and the Swedish Security Service confirmed it had been sabotage.

Shortly after the war in Ukraine began, media censorship started on both sides, using different techniques. Outlets like *Le Monde* from Paris ("*In Latin America, the Pro-Putin Accents of the Left*") portrayed Paco Ignacio Taibo and me as examples of a Latin American left that blames NATO for the war because, according to this well-known technique of demonization and psychological discrediting, we blame everything that comes from Washington. Which is not true, because "leftist intellectuals" like me support all social plans in the United States and believe this country will achieve peace when it awakens from its war and monetary nightmares. We do not support the omnipresent business of war and its powerful media arm.

My opinion is irrelevant, but the attacks are significant and symptomatic. I never stopped clarifying that I did not support an invasion of Ukraine by Moscow, purely on principle: I cannot support any war, least of all a preventive one. Perhaps that's why, after more than a decade of frequent collaboration with RT TV, we never scheduled another interview. On the other hand, warning about the powerful Western war propaganda and the non-existent space given to those who criticize and hold NATO accountable is another form of censorship—very effective and classic of the so-called "Free World."

The greatest threat to the American people are the owners of the United States (megacorporations, megalomaniac politicians, captured media, and what President and General Eisenhower called in 1961 "the danger of the Military Industrial Complex") down to their happy slaves (gun and war enthusiasts, fanatical addicts, the homeless but evangelized capitalists).

On February 8, 2023, journalist Seymour Hersh published the now well-known article claiming that the sabotage of Nord Stream in September 2022 was a CIA operation. The White House labeled it as "pure fiction," despite the fact that exactly one year earlier, President Biden had warned that "if Russia invades... there will no longer be a Nord Stream II; we will take care of it." Seven months later, the pipelines of Nord Stream II exploded again.

Was the urgent and chaotic withdrawal from Afghanistan related to the sabotage of Nord Stream II? I have no proof, but no doubts either. In thirty years, documents will be declassified proving that Washington and the CIA already had plans for the war in Ukraine and needed to move the multi-trillion-dollar resources from the opium country to a new war aimed at cornering China, another invented enemy before it even existed.

As always, in the name of Peace, Freedom, and Democracy.

Who is stuck in the Cold War?

Le Monde published a lengthy indictment against "leftist intellectuals" who do not approve of Putin's invasion but hold NATO responsible for provoking the conflict. Paco Ignacio Taibo II was accused of denouncing "the new censorship against Russian publishers by the International Book Fair" in Guadalajara, which also does not mean he approves of Russia's censorship of Western media.

As for me, the French outlet dismissed me with a sample of superficial interpretations like: "In a series of opinion articles published in the Argentine newspaper *Página 12*, the Uruguayan intellectual Jorge Majfud voices this left that remains very discreet on the issue, and explains 'why much of the world's left supports Putin [who] is too clever for the leaders of the West,' he says, pulling the thread of the anti-NATO and anti-US stance with the idea that 'The only argument hegemon powers understand is atomic bombs."

In a subtitle, it repeats and highlights: "The Russian war, 'unfortunately simple, is a reaction to actions largely taken by Washington,' writes the Uruguayan intellectual..." etc.

Neither the voice of the left nor discreet, let alone timid. Tell that to those who threaten and accuse us of being *radicals*, simply for not aligning ourselves with either the warmongering radicalism of the 'good guys' or the double standards that lead to deplorable figures like Condoleezza Rice to claim that the invasion "violates international laws." Or to the even more despicable George Bush, who condemned Putin for launching a war "unprovoked and unjustified." Or to President Joe Biden, declaring Putin to be "a war criminal," a title he would never accept for any former president of his country.

Let alone the classic double standards of the polished racists who, magically, opened Europe's borders to welcome Ukrainian refugees—a policy perfectly correct if it weren't for the fact that those same borders were closed to those fleeing the chaos of Africa and the Middle East, chaos produced by invasions, plunder, massacres, and wars waged by the Northwestern powers for the past couple of centuries. Let alone the magical border opening of Washington to welcome 100.000 Ukrainian refugees, or the reports of the ease with which Ukrainians find crossing the border into Mexico, the same border that was always closed to refugees from the south; children and women, refugees from the chaos created by Washington in Central America, the Caribbean, and beyond, with its dictatorships and massacres long before the

Cold War, during, and after. As is the case with Haiti, block-aded and ruined since it became the first free country in the Americas in 1804, and bled dry until just yesterday by France, by the Duvalier dictatorships, by the terror of CIA paramili-taries, the coups against Aristide, or the neoliberal imposi-tion that ruined the country, to cite just one example. When these people fled the chaos, they were hunted down like criminals. In 2021, we witnessed the hunting of Haitians at the border, on horseback, as slaves were hunted in the 19th century.

More direct were the journalists from Western networks who reported the tragedy of Ukrainians as something unac-ceptable, given they are "Christian white people," "civilized people," "blue-eyed blondes." Or politicians, like Poland's ruling party member Dominik Tarczyński, who proudly con-firmed they were open to Ukrainian immigration because they were "peaceful people" but would not accept a single Muslim refugee. "Zero." As for violent Nazi leaders like Ar-tiom Bonov, refugees in their own country, silence.

As an example to follow, *Le Monde* praised "the young Chilean president, Gabriel Boric" who "unequivocally con-demned the invasion of Ukraine, the violation of its sover-eignty, and the illegitimate use of force." In other words, if one doesn't understand that reality is a football game and that one must be one hundred percent on one side without criticizing the other, it's because one is on one side without criticizing the other.

Not by chance, imperial powers for generations have not accepted being labeled as such. For them, it's not the time to mention Western imperialism. It's never a good time to talk about imperialism, except when another military power dares to do the same thing.

Le Monde nuances when quoting me again on something we've been saying for months before the war: "That we consider NATO the main responsible for the conflict in Ukraine does not mean we support Putin, nor any war…" But in their line of thinking, this is merely an irrelevant detail. The thesis is different: criticism of NATO is due to the fact that "Anti-Americanism remains rooted in the subcontinent." Like the old and childish argument that (in the Sub) "they hate us because we are rich and free."

Recently, University of Chicago professor and regional expert John Mearsheimer, in The Economist and The New Yorker, blamed the United States for the war in Ukraine. A few days ago, Noam Chomsky reminded me that not only had he warned years ago about the danger of war by not maintaining Ukraine's neutrality, but also "George Kennan, Henry Kissinger, the CIA director and practically the entire higher diplomatic corps who knew something about the region were of the same opinion. It's madness."

Madness, but it has an explanation: the boundless greed of the merchants of death, the same one that President and General Eisenhower warned in his farewell speech as a greater danger to democracy and the policies of the United States.

Now, that we agree with Kissinger and the CIA on the causes of the conflict, does not mean we agree on the objectives. An example I've outlined in The Savage Border sums it all up: the CIA inoculated in Latin American populations the idea that fascist dictatorships in Latin America were to combat communism, and that, for example, Salvador Allende would turn Chile into a new Cuba, while their agents and analysts reported the opposite: had they done nothing, it was most likely that, due to Washington's policy of ruining the Chilean economy, Allende would have lost the next election. But the goal was to create a neoliberal laboratory under the tutelage of a dictatorship, as so many other times. The CIA promoted in the major Latin American press and even on the streets with flyers and posters a narrative they didn't believe in and even laughed at. Even today, the non-existent "communist threat" is repeated with fanaticism by their stewards, from pro-oligarchic politicians to the press and their honorary and mercenary journalists.

To get a sense of how this media manipulation continues, it's enough to consider that Western secret agencies have budgets several times larger than they had in 1950 or 1990, and they don't just use them to train neo-Nazi militias in Ukraine, which they called, as in so many other countries, "self-defense forces." Self-defense forces that failed to prevent a Russian invasion or even what President Zelensky now wants to negotiate, Russia's first demand: Ukraine's neutrality.

So, are the leftist critics the ones trapped in the Cold War, or is it the mercenaries of big capital, NATO, and the multiple imperialist interventions?

Why does a large part of the left support Putin

Beyond his reasons for intervening in Ukraine, Putin poses an ideological challenge to 20th-century standards. A conservative, but anti-Nazi. A capitalist in his own way.

The fact that the global left supports him lies in his shrewd and powerful response to the economic and military hegemony of the West. Standing up to centuries of arrogance in the name of democracy and freedom is no small thing. Democracy and freedom that the countries invaded by Western superpowers never saw. Quite the opposite. Just as in the times of slavery, when the Southern Democrats of the United States stole territories from Mexico to expand this dehumanizing system, it was always done in the name of civilization and freedom. The same occurred after its legal abolition: throughout the entire 20th century, invasions, coups d'état, and friendly dictatorships were spread across all continents in the name of freedom and democracy. More recently, the struggle for Human Rights was added to the very short menu of positive, yet criminal, ideolexicons.

If there was some measure of freedom, democracy, and human rights in Europe and the United States (far more than in the colonies and neocolonies friendly to and functional for their economic interests), it was not due to any of the brutal and arrogant military interventions and economic blockades against non-aligned countries. It would suffice to consider that the Vietnam War, "to protect our freedoms" as many in the United States repeat, was an expensive but scandalous defeat. Except in movies and social discourse. Aside from another fiasco for the greatest military power and the millions of Vietnamese massacred under 7.5 million tons of bombs and as many tons of Agent Orange, no American lost any "freedom." On the contrary, they gained a few. The only concrete freedoms that were achieved were the result of the struggle of the demonized, unpatriotic Civil Rights activists, like the socialist (shhh, don't say it) Martin Luther King or the rebellious boxer and anti-war activist Muhammad Ali ("I won't go to kill people on the other side of the world; my enemies are not the Vietnamese but you, the white oppressors").

In every single case where the West gained some new freedom ("equal-freedom," not the freedom of the slaveholder to enslave others), it was thanks to the demonized leftist movements, the heroic mobilizations of those at the bottom, whose achievements were systematically hijacked by conservatives when there was no turning back, or the vindication of returning to the "good old days" of conservatives had to wait until the propaganda of those at the top, those at the center, had some effect on those at the bottom, those on the periphery.

I believe this historical logic explains the apparent ideological contradictions in an event that is now shaking the world, namely Russia's military intervention in Ukraine. Back to the beginning: aside from Putin's reasons for intervening (the expansion of NATO, the massacres in Donbas), the meaning of the intervention has deep global historical roots and is a sign that we are approaching the Thucydides Trap—but we've already been discussing this for a couple of decades.

Bush, Putin, and Newton's Third Law

"For every action, there is an equal and opposite reaction," would be the summary of Newton's third law. This law of classical physics is fundamental in the social and political dynamics of nations, with the difference that the reaction is never proportional to the action. If we add the golden rule of diplomacy and humanity's oldest moral law ("Do unto others as you would have them do unto you"), we will have the explanation for many phenomena throughout history and across the present.

To begin, let's take just one element, the rhetorical one, concerning the two major military interventions of the last generation: the invasion of Iraq and the invasion of Ukraine.

On Monday, March 17, 2003, from the Cross Hall of the White House, the then U.S. president delivered a speech justifying the massive invasion of Iraq. A month earlier, from Spain, we had published articles taking this invasion for granted, as well as the subsequent quagmire in the chaos of the Middle East. At the time, we thought the speech was a blatant lie. Today, after the admission of its falsehood, both by resident Bush and his shield-bearer, President Aznar, it is clear that it was all a fabrication. As clear as it is nearly impossible to find an American who is aware of these facts.

The speech stated:

"For more than a decade, the United States and other nations have pursued patient and honorable efforts to disarm the Iraqi regime without resorting to war(but) *they have failed time and time again"*. In reality, UN inspectors only failed in their search for weapons of mass destruction.

"The intelligence gathered by this and other governments leaves no doubt that the Iraqi regime continues to possess and conceal some of the most lethal weapons ever devised(...) *The regime has a history of aggression in the Middle East* and harbors a deep hatred for the United States and our allies. And it has aided, trained, and harbored terrorists, including agents of Al Qaeda." We all know it was the CIA who aided and trained Osama bin Laden in Afghanistan. Saddam Hussein was bin Laden's enemy. We also knew that the regime's "history of aggression" was backed by Washington, even with biological weapons sold by Europe in the 80s and approved by Ronald Reagan.

"The United States and other nations did nothing to deserve this threat". Surely not. Now, *"the decades of deceit and cruelty have come to an end. Saddam Hussein* and his sons must leave Iraq within 48 hours. Their refusal to do so will result in a

military conflict, which will begin at a time of our choosing. For their own safety, all foreign citizens, including journalists and inspectors, must leave Iraq immediately (…) The military campaign will be directed against the lawless men who rule their country and not against the Iraqi people (…) We call on the Iraqi armed forces to act honorably and protect their country by allowing the peaceful entry of coalition forces to eliminate weapons of mass destruction. (…) War criminals will be punished. And it will be no defense to say 'I was only following orders.'"

"We will continue to take further measures to protect our homeland. Our enemies will fail. None of their actions can alter the course or change the determination of this nation. We are a peaceful people (…) If our enemies dare to attack us, they will face terrible consequences. Unlike Saddam Hussein, we believe the Iraqi people deserve and are capable of being free. And when the dictator is gone, they can set an example for the entire Middle East of a vital, peaceful, and autonomous nation. The United States, alongside other countries, will work to promote freedom and peace in that region."

On February 23, 2022, Russian president Vladimir Putin announced his decision to launch a "special military operation" to defend a separatist province in Ukraine.

"I have made the decision to carry out a special military operation to protect the people who have been subjected to abuse and genocide by the Kyiv regime for eight years. To this end, we will strive to demilitarize and denazify Ukraine. And also to bring to justice those who have committed numerous bloody crimes against

the civilian population, including citizens of the Russian Federation. Russia cannot exist under constant threat emanating from Ukrainian territory. We have been left with no other option."

To make it more akin to Bush's speech, as if it were a deliberate rhetorical device:

"*Today's events are not related to the desire to harm the interests of Ukraine and the Ukrainian people, but rather to protect Russia from those who have taken Ukraine hostage and seek to use it against our people.*" It is about "*the right to defend ourselves against the threats of even greater calamity than the present one. Our plans do not include the occupation of Ukrainian territories, nor will we impose anything on anyone by force. Our policy is based on freedom(…)It is important that all peoples living on the territory of present-day Ukraine be able to exercise this right: the right to choose freely.*"

For the enemies who dare to attack, Putin, as Bush did, warns them that they will face terrible consequences:

"*A direct attack on Russia would lead to defeat and dire consequences for the potential aggressor (…) Not a single day passes without bombings in the towns of Donbas(…)The slaughter of civilians does not stop, nor does the harassment of people, including children, women, and the elderly(…)They have left us no other opportunity to protect Russia, our people, except the one we will be forced to use today*".

The two speeches that initiated both military interventions are almost identical. It is possible that this was deliberate on Moscow's part, but it is clear that it is a diplomatic and military reaction of crucial importance. Washington's arrogance in not stopping the expansion of NATO, against commitments made decades ago and repeatedly violated, has crashed into the Russian wall (or rather, the "Sino-Russian" wall).

Putin is too clever for Western leaders. Moreover, he is at the breaking point of NATO's overwhelming influence and its decline. The examples of military inefficiency of the most expensive army in history (the U.S. spends as much as the top ten countries in the world) are endless. From the expansionist wars of the 19th century, through the banana wars and all Cold War invasions, tiny or poor countries were always invaded or intervened in. Even so, they were defeated in Cuba, Vietnam, and, more recently, in Afghanistan. Now, in the face of the imminent invasion of Ukraine by the Russian army, Washington withdrew its military presence from Ukraine. After all, that's what they were there for—to intimidate.

Even if Putin withdraws from Ukraine, even if he stays with a part or invents a new country, he will be the inevitable winner in this dispute. The lesson had already been learned by Kim Jong-un after Saddam Hussein was hanged: the only argument that hegemonic powers listen to is atomic bombs.

Sadly, it's that simple, and that is another reaction to a policy long exercised by Washington.

The War Within Us

In 2021, we published that, following Washington's costly defeat in Afghanistan, we had to prepare for a new war; that long before China, a conflict with Russia would come. When the new war finally arrived, we tried to understand it. Apart from donations that are like aspirins every time a country is invaded, the importance of our dialectical efforts, no matter how important the medium in which they are published, is equally irrelevant.

There is a reality that occupies neither the Greeks nor the Trojans in the international media: the war we all carry within, which, to a large extent, explains part of this war and all political wars. Some will tell me that this belongs to psychology, that I shouldn't delve into such topics. Well, in the more than 530 articles I've published since the neoliberal catastrophe in Latin America in the late 1990s, I've always practiced the illegal profession of essayist.

To summarize, let's take a couple of cases among thousands. As someone once said long ago, I'm going to start by talking about myself, since that's who I'm closest to.

In early 2017, friends from a Spanish outlet I collaborated with for many years asked me to comment on the conflict in Catalonia. I insisted that, aside from being an enthusiast of Spanish culture and its tragic history, I was neither then nor now an expert on Catalonia, and that, from my external perspective, the Catalans should be allowed to hold their referendum on the debated independence, as Scotland did in 2014. A non-binding referendum, like the one Manuel Zelaya tried to hold in Honduras. As a result, just as with the case of Honduras, I lost several friends. Let's call them that, "friends," though everyone knows real friends aren't lost over political differences. Thus, in a few hours, I went from being, for years, "the most important intellectual in Latin America" to the category of "idiot." In both cases, they were exaggerating, though about the latter, one can never be entirely sure.

Exactly the same has happened with the conflict in Ukraine. My position, as in the case of Catalonia, is not radical at all. Again, I admit and acknowledge that I'm no expert on Ukraine. I only try to contribute an external perspective, based on my limited historical and global knowledge (isn't this conflict just a historical-geopolitical clash?).

On the very day of Putin's invasion, I published in several newspapers a comparison between Bush's speech before invading Iraq and Putin's speech before invading Ukraine. Of course, there are significant factual differences, but at the time I understood, and still understand, that Putin was sending a message with the rhetorical parallel. Accusations of Russophobia were quick to follow. Soon after, at the request of a couple of editors, I sent other pieces, with similar results: I was a "leftist" justifying the deaths of hundreds of Ukrainians by mentioning NATO's responsibility in advance toward Russia's border, the Ukrainian massacres in Donbas, the Nazi paramilitarism of the Azov Battalion, censorship in Western media, and the double standard in judging other invasions and massacres that are not just history but the present, like Palestine, Iraq, Afghanistan, Libya, Syria, Yemen, Somalia... "It's not the time to talk about Western imperialism because Ukrainian victims are suffering"; "Racism against black refugees from Ukraine?"; "It's not the time to mention open-border policies for blond people and closed borders for those from Africa or the Middle East; you're just playing into Putin's hands."

While all criticism is respectable, a large proportion of the comments not only showed that their authors hadn't carefully read each article (right or wrong), but they were arguing against points that weren't there or repeating accusations that were already addressed Certainly, in large part, this could be due to the shortcomings of each article itself. It's not easy to be clear when you have to say everything in fewer than a thousand words, as if you were Maradona shaking off two opponents and delivering a rabona cross, all in a single tile.

Up to this point, fine. All of this is part of a necessary dynamic for any democracy, for any maturity of the freedom of peoples. Thinking differently is human nature, and that's not what we wish to correct in ourselves. The problem (a case study) arises when political disagreements end years-long friendships. That's where we have a global problem, and the conflict zone is just a stage for personal angers and frustrations. Especially when it comes to unforeseen conflicts that reposition many people. When Russia bombed Chechnya and in a few years caused the death of 50,000 civilians, it inflamed almost no one's chest. Palestinians, Iraqis, or Afghans "are all terrorists" and "don't have blue eyes." The same goes for countless other massacres committed by Western powers. We're used to it; our opinions surprise no one.

As in the case of Catalonia, with Ukraine I lost several friends. I repeat, it's not that it's something important, because true friends aren't lost over differences of opinion; nor is this a conflict about which I've had firm opinions for years. What matters, I think, is the psychological state we're all immersed in, one that closely resembles the moment when a drunk's euphoria begins to descend the bell curve and transforms into an overwhelming urge to fight whoever crosses their path.

Of course, none of this is coincidental. Conflicts over opinions have always existed, and even in the past, a different interpretation of the sex of angels was enough to end in a massacre in civilized Paris, like the St. Bartholomew's Day massacre. But after several centuries of social progress based on the struggle for *equal-liberty*, more recently we've been losing ground. The rise of fascism and Nazism are merely symptoms of a larger reality: the hijacking of humanity's progress by the owners of the means (productive means; means of information).

Old story. In this too, social media is playing a decisive role: bringing us closer, but not infrequently like someone on a highway who approaches other drivers—going the wrong way. Largely, it boils down to social engineering. A few are capitalizing on all this hatred, and they're doing it very well. Is it too hard to guess where secret agencies are investing trillions of dollars, for example, with mega software like Pegasus, those caves of true power that have no faces like Biden or Putin and do everything in the name of Security and Defense? Well, nothing else but politics, because that's the weapon of the 21st century. World War III has already begun in cyberspace, and it's far more powerful than any army and those jokes of elite soldiers trained to endure five minutes underwater.

The rest of us have an invisible but global problem. This war will pass, and others will come, and the guilty won't just be Bush or Saddam Hussein, Obama, Osama, Biden, Putin, or Rasputin, but people very much like them who think they're better than them only because they don't have the destructive power they wield: us, hating each other, divided, manipulated, and fighting the wrong war.

Another war that's not ours.

The dictatorship of the media

We'll have to repeat it endlessly: considering NATO as the primary responsible party for the conflict in Ukraine doesn't mean we support Putin or any war.

Nor do we support the global media dictatorship and its crocodile tears.

It's part of a strategy in which even the most honest people fall: if you're against NATO's imperialism, you're in favor
of Putin's war. Or don't mention our imperialism because
innocent people are dying in Ukraine. Well, imperialism
must always be remembered, because it's shy and doesn't
want to be mentioned, because, though not absolute, it's the
main political and ideological framework of the world, and
it's even more important to mention it now because it poses
as the altruistic defender of Ukrainian victims, while being a
direct protagonist in this tragedy.

Consequently, the soccer effect works perfectly. And this
isn't just a metaphor: the old mafia of FIFA has suspended
Russia's soccer team from this year's World Cup in Qatar, a
tournament where human rights are conspicuously absent.
FIFA was able to hold World Cups in fascist dictatorships,
like Argentina in 1978 or fascist Italy in 1934, manipulated
in favor of Mussolini's regime (Il Duce also intervened in
France 1938). Three cases that ended with the winning of the
ultimate trophy, where not only the players were victims but
those events served as moral legitimization for barbarity.
FIFA also knew how to maintain "sporting neutrality" during more recent massacres. The big sports TV chains had
never broadcast with the banner "No to War" until now. But
among mafiosos, they defend each other.

In the same vein of pseudo ideological neutrality, major
global platforms, such as social networks (always but increasingly more evident), have self-proclaimed themselves judges
of global truth and label all news from outlets like Russia TV

with the warning "this news comes from a media outlet affiliated with the Russian government." Even banana republic governments have censored this news channel, despite the fact that no one ever dared to do anything similar with CNN and Fox News when they enabled the misinformation that ended with the massacre of a million people in Iraq and half a continent plunged into a bloody chaos that still persists.

Not to mention the classic censorship of visibility and media positioning by Internet search engines that maintain an almost absolute oligopoly, all manipulated from San Francisco.

Our position on this issue hasn't changed now. When, a few years ago, Twitter canceled Donald Trump's account, even though we considered it a cesspool of trash, we opposed that. Freedom of expression (on steroids for the owners of money and limited by the job vulnerability of those at the bottom) means that even those who think radically differently from us have the right to say it. It's the people who must mature and educate themselves to learn to digest information and, above all, learn to organize so as not to leave the majority of the most powerful media, the creators of fear and opinion, always in the hands of the owners of capital. Why do four or five powerful CEOs of mega-corporations, chosen by no one but their tiny council of cardinals, proclaim themselves guardians of the truth?

Of course, in all other cases, they neither label nor mention the affiliations of Western media with aligned governments. Major opinion-creating chains, like Fox News or

CNN, responsible for supporting massive wars and conceal-
ing their crimes against humanity, are no more independent
by being private; on the contrary: their empires don't depend
on readers but on their millionaire advertisers and the powerful interests of their micro social class. Their news should
be preceded with the warning: "this media is affiliated with
or responds to the special interests of lobbies, corporations
and transnationals."

To a large extent, channels that don't hide their affiliation to a government, union, or ideology are more honest
than those with international projection and devastating influence who pose as independent champions of informa-
tional objectivity.

Moreover, media objectivity doesn't exist, and neutrality
is mere cowardice, if not cynicism. What exists and should
be appreciated is honesty, acknowledging once and for all
whose worldview we support and whether that vision depends on our personal interests, class interests, or something
broader called humanity.

Google, YouTube, and the *Moralfare*

In March 2022, one month after the start of the war in
Ukraine, the giant Google, owner of YouTube, warned content producers (though with cosmetic rights, they are the
main employees of the super platform; those who achieve at
least 1,000 subscribers and 4,000 hours of views receive their
first dollar) to be careful with their audiovisual products and

refrain from expressing any idea or opinion that *"exploits, dis-regards, or approves"* the war in Ukraine.

Naturally, none of these warnings were ever enacted for NATO-led wars, not even the most recent ones in the Middle East and North Africa. On the contrary, the brutal invasion of Iraq based on "false information" and childlike narratives, which left a million dead, millions displaced, and half a continent plunged into the most violent chaos imaginable, was supported by these same media based, for example, on the "Patriot Act" approved in Washington in October 2001, which didn't even allow publishing photos of their own dead returning to the country or the foreign dead sinking into oblivion; on the other hand, it required that every report "from the scene of events" be accompanied by the repeated reference to the attack on the Twin Towers. Not to mention more recent wars, massacres, systematic drone bombings, killings hidden from public opinion, inoculated or hijacked rebellions, assassinations of dictators or rebel leaders, like Muammar Gaddafi's., and ongoing human rights violations by powerful governments, such as the abuses and mass exterminations of peoples in Yemen, Syria, and Palestine.

A subtle and highly effective form of censorship against small and large producers of cultural, entertainment, or news content on YouTube consisted of the best censorship strategy any democratic or dictatorial system has known in recent centuries, from the Panopticon of Jeremy Bentham in the 18th century to the fear among users that the CIA or the NSA and other secret agencies are monitoring their activities on the Internet, including countless dictatorships, such as the military-capitalist dictatorships in Latin America during the 20th century.

In this case, self-censorship began with the threat, by Google and YouTube, of *demonetization*. That is, you are free to think whatever you want, but if you say something we disagree with, we will stop paying you for your work, and there is no union that can defend you. In fact, that is what happened to many independent journalists on the platform, some of whom are my friends.

In other words, the mega-platforms, born and legally based in the United States, do not even respect their own country's constitution, which, in its First Amendment, guarantees freedom of expression, regardless of whether it is the expression of the KKK or the Nazis, neo-Nazis, and re-Nazis. This results in a serious contradiction to the extraterritorial reach of the same U.S. laws that are applied even in countries like China, in the facilities of companies like Apple or Microsoft, as if they had diplomatic immunity.

Google capped its threat with the following moral sermon, typical of the double standards of great powers and large corporations: the company's policies are violated when, for example, "dangerous or derogatory content… that incites violence or denies tragic events" in Ukraine is published. If there is a lawfare for dissidents, there is a *moralfare* (especially in private companies that write their own laws) to hijack principles dear to those at the bottom.

The victims are victims in any case (from the Sahara to Madrid, from Libya to Paris, from South Africa and the Congo to London and Brussels, from Guatemala and Chile to Washington, from Syria and Palestine to Ukraine), but the *moralfare* is used only to pity and support with the full force of the media, propaganda, and international narrative some victims while invisibilizing others.

The mafia of corporations of the First World is a global octopus with tentacles, and they all have one thing in common: money, media, and power. Russia's selection was excluded from the 2022 World Cup in Qatar, without anyone being horrified by the 7,000 immigrant deaths caused by preparing the global football party in that Persian Gulf petrodictatorship, where, as in Saudi Arabia, there is no room for the outrage of oppressed women or the outrage of NATO women for media and strategic reasons. FIFA itself was complicit in the Italian fascism that made winning the football championships in 1934 and 1938 possible; the same case as Argentina in 1978, when the brutal dictatorship of General Videla was not punished but rewarded by the international mafia. The United States participated in the 2002 World Cup in South Korea and Japan, despite the massive bombings, tortures, and massacres in Iraq.

In 2011, Sevilla footballer Frederic Kanouté was sanctioned for showing his support for the Palestinian people. As soon as the war in Ukraine began, all broadcasts of matches in the popular and powerful Spanish La Liga were relentlessly accompanied by a Ukrainian flag next to the timer, as a sign of solidarity with the aggression by a stronger country (the media reports a war of *Russia against Ukraine*, not the more obvious war of *Russia against NATO*). European football clubs, like Atlético de Madrid, illuminated their stadiums with the colors of the Ukrainian flag, for which they received congratulations for their act of heroism and solidarity with Human Rights. The same occurred in other stadiums, like England's Wembley. In many matches of the equally powerful English Premier League, players were forced to enter the field with the Ukrainian flag, as a sign of sporting neutrality.

As established and practiced by the father of modern propaganda, Edward Bernays, the best way to manage a democracy is by telling citizens what to think. "The conscious and intelligent manipulation of the organized habits and opinions of the masses is an important element in a democratic society." According to a report by the American Civil Liberties Union (ACLU) published in 2022, "the U.S. Supreme Court acknowledged in 1936 that 'an informed public is the most powerful of all restraints against government abuses. Yet, today, much of our government's business is conducted in secret. There exists a multitude of secret agencies, secret congressional committees, secret courts, and even secret laws. This ever-expanding secret state represents a serious threat to individual liberty and undermines the very notion of government of, by, and for the people."

A WhatsApp about the war[3]

"Good morning, Dr. Majfud. I'm Xxx from the news channel BBNN. Hhh from XYZ gave me your number. We wanted to know if you're available for an interview tomorrow at 9:00 in the morning."

"Will it be recorded? Could it be at 7:00 AM here?"

"Yes, that works. We'll talk about the invasion of Ukraine, Russia's expulsion from the UN Human Rights Council, and the calls to put Putin on trial for war crimes."

"OK. Will we also discuss Mosul and other war crimes committed by NATO?"

"The idea is to focus on what's current. Do you agree with the invasion of Ukraine?"

"I've said it a thousand times: no, I don't agree. An Isaac Newton has claimed that I write what I write because I'm pro-Putin and that I don't understand reality. The expert is British, though he's done some tourism in Poland."

"Are you with Putin?"

"Again? Where do you get that? Do I look like Putin? I also don't agree with NATO. Look, I don't claim to own the truth, but I'm against the double standards of the superpowers and against media manipulation. Is that bad? Isn't it time to criticize the double standards of the superpowers? When,

---

[3] Chat corrected in punctuation and slightly modified to preserve the privacy of the channel's producer.

if not now? Should I say what others want so as not to offend anyone? Why are you so concerned about the opinion of someone like me, with zero influence in these conflicts?"

"Now is not the time to talk about past invasions... In journalism, we have little time and must focus on the news."

"That's the problem. Does anyone believe that journalism, even the best and most honest, is a neutral mirror of reality? Besides, these aren't just past invasions or tragedies. We're talking about war crimes from recent decades in several "unimportant" countries but on a larger scale. Look at what's happening right now in Yemen or Palestine... A couple of months ago, over 200 people were massacred in Saada and Hodeidah, Yemen, by Saudi airplanes and American bombs. Nothing compared to the 300,000 who have already died before. Mostly children and young people, though not blonde or blue-eyed. Do you remember Saada and Hodeidah? Did you do a program to express outrage at that massacre? Turns out it's never the time to talk about the crimes of the good guys. When, then? If you want my modest opinion, I'd rather talk about the whole movie, not just one scene. Is there any scene in any movie that makes sense without the preceding ones?"

"Mr. Majfud, this isn't the medium to discuss such complex issues."

"No, of course not. I was just giving you some material to plan the interview. That's what you always ask for. Can we discuss it during the interview, even briefly?"

There was no response or interview. As the producers of a Latin American network that used to call me until ten years ago used to say when they didn't like what I was saying, "Sorry, professor, we're having technical issues." The last time, I think it was in 2014 or 2015 in the middle of a debate, I was cut off before I could finish my reply to the analysts in the studio." (The network was NTN24; in this case, I can say it because the dialogue didn't take place in a private medium.)

"Excuse me, Mr. Majfud, we're having technical issues," the producer told me.

"What a coincidence," I said, "just when I thought we were going to have technical issues."

That was the last time they called me. And so many others that call themselves *media*: half-truths, half-objective, half-independent.

The Double Standards of Western Propaganda

Without defending censorship in various countries of the East and the colonized South (quite the opposite, but sometimes it needs to be clarified for some schoolchildren), let's add another example of how the propaganda of Western powers operates, always so proud of their freedom whenever they look in Narcissus's mirror.

Voice of America (VOA), which, along with TV Martí and other channels (their names include terms like Free or

Liberty), is a branch of the U.S. Agency for Global Media funded by the U.S. government. It was founded in 1941, initially with the noble goal of countering Nazi propaganda, a direct offspring of American propaganda, just as Joseph Goebbels was inspired by Edward Bernays and Hitler by Madison Grant.

Since then, VOA hasn't stopped operating in dozens of countries, especially during the Cold War and afterward, "to promote democratic values." Beyond the slogans, VOA is a well-known propaganda media conglomerate that in the past served to prepare for hard coups, with invasions or direct military interventions. Today, its budget, coming from the U.S. government, is in the hundreds of millions of dollars, and it operates in various countries shaping public opinion.

It has also been one of the media extensions of the CIA. Like the Agency, VOA is a permanent organization and, in theory, isn't designed to operate on U.S. soil but in the rest of the world. It belongs to what is classified as "white propaganda," meaning non-secret propaganda, but in such a way that it doesn't seem like propaganda. Examples of "black propaganda," used and abused by the Agency and the private corporations of the First World, are abundant in the recent history of the erroneously called Third World.

Like media funded by foreign governments, VOA defines itself as "independent of the government" of the United States that funds it. No one would expect otherwise from a medium that presents itself as a champion of truth, freedom, and independence from all ideology or political power. Of course, as in any other case, it's reasonable to assume that at some point some journalists have exercised their freedom against the dominant ideology. But, like the op-eds in major media, it's only a moral tax that non-democratic corporations must pay to consider themselves democratic or, at least, tolerate and adapt to a complex, contradictory, and relatively open society, as some Western societies still are, thanks mainly to their dissidents, those who refuse to resign themselves to the idea that countries have owners, are armies, tribes, or sects.

It's enough to conduct a micro-experiment by sharing any of VOA's reports on social media. Massive creators of collective opinion like Twitter don't warn, as in other cases of media funded by non-aligned governments (TeleSur from Venezuela, RT from Russia, or some public media from China), that "this medium is funded by the government of…"

This is what is called *Free Press*, which, apart from media funded by Washington, also includes other private and more powerful conglomerates, free from any suspicion of having special interests, like CNN, Fox News, and a long list of mercenaries shaping the Free Opinion of the People—whichever people that may be.

The Most Dangerous Game in the World

While, on one hand, major media worldwide endlessly reproduce horrifying images of hundreds of corpses scattered in Bucha, Ukraine, on the other hand, they fan the flames of a military escalation that could lead us in months to nuclear holocaust.

Whoever committed that massacre (it seems most likely it was the Russian soldiers) will go down in the annals of history as an unforgivable crime. But I believe the smoke obscures the horizon. We can't see where we come from and, worse, we can't see where we're headed. Although I've repeated it in different media long before the war, right or wrong, I'm going to insist on those two sides of the path that the fire prevents us from seeing.

Let's start with a simple and more immediate question: instead of continuing the endless, dangerous, and notoriously futile game of arbitrary sanctions, why not impose the obligation to negotiate a resolution to the conflict between Russia and NATO once and for all, before more innocents die?

A reasonable solution would be the dissolution of NATO in exchange for Russia's withdrawal from Ukraine, but that would be labeled as radical. The owners of the business don't negotiate.

There are many other options, such as the most obvious and pragmatic one, namely Ukraine's neutral status (with provincial autonomy for Donbas), which is where we should have started instead of provoking Russia by integrating Ukraine into NATO and deploying missiles four minutes from Moscow.

Neutrality or non-membership in NATO has always been the case for Austria, Finland, Sweden, and other neighboring countries, some of which have recently expressed the possibility of joining NATO, showing where the business of the old war merchants is headed and demonstrating, once again, that not only in Latin America the fight against communism was nothing more than the perfect excuse to maintain geopolitical dominance and protect corporate, class, and capital interests.

What do they aim for, apart from expanding militarization more and more in a world now that the excuse of communism and, more recently, Islamic terrorism has run out, the latter alone in Afghanistan leaving eight trillion dollars in profits for major companies specialized in "security"?

Do they think a Russia surrounded by that anachronistic and mafia-like organization, NATO, would make Europe and the world a safer place?

One must be under the influence of alcohol to forget that we're talking about one of the two nuclear superpowers and to imagine such stupidity. Or such evil by organized crime. If it were truly about "security," if they were sincere about the "right to defend themselves" that countries have, they would never have attempted to disrupt this order which, judging by the ongoing war, has not made the world safer at all, quite the opposite. Much less Ukraine.

Of course, those with the power to negotiate are not being splattered with the blood of Russians and Ukrainians but, on the contrary, are doing their business, so it may take them weeks, if not months, to stop shedding crocodile tears over their whiskey and start negotiating seriously.

THE DANGER OF CULTURE

It's the culture, idiot

In March 2023, the principal of a high school in Tallahassee, Florida, was removed after she showed Michelangelo's David in her art class. Some parents accused Carrasquilla of exposing their innocent teenagers to pornographic material, and the school board gave her two options: resign or be fired.

A month earlier, in my Architecture and Civilization class, I projected the same David and I withhold comments on a couple of reactions. I will continue to include in the program for the coming years relevant examples from human history that would be considered "explicit adult material," such as Indian architecture, Greek pottery, and Gothic cathedrals (Christian paradigms of conservative Europe) with their gargoyles draining rainwater from their vaginas.

Now we better understand why Goya painted the Maja clothed after achieving a better work with the same woman naked a few years earlier; he surely didn't want to be censored in Florida two hundred years later.

What still saves me is that I teach at a university, and in the past when these complaints have come my way, it's been enough with a couple of sarcastic remarks and a firm stance. I published an article on this very topic in 2005 titled "The

Immo(rality) of Art, the Evil of the Poor" about a class at the University of Georgia.

Not One Step Back in the Demonization of Culture, because it is culture, not pornography, that fanatics truly fear and hate: pornography is a business; culture is a danger that can open even the hardest and most closed minds. Radical culture is naturally rebellious and subversive. Of the real pornography that teenagers and even children in secondary schools watch on their phones, not a word; but laws banning books on racism and revisionist history abound.

This is where we've arrived in Florida. If we previously warned of a movement towards the Middle Ages (toward the most brutal fanaticism of the Middle Ages and the Inquisition), it must be said that we've already been there for a while.

The Strategy of Forgetting

Since the end of 2022, it has become recurrent in U.S. media to make a list of all the lies that Republican Representative George Santos of New York put on his resume and repeated every chance he got. However, fragile popular memory either doesn't record or quickly forgets that this has been a fairly common practice, though rarely as caricaturesque as Santos's. As everyone knows, one of the most common ways is to lie by hiding part of the truth. A part so important that it deserves to be hidden or, at best, repressed.

In political advertising in the state of Florida, for example, it's common to see candidates posing with their children and stating that their father "escaped the communist regime of Cuba seeking the freedom of this Great Country." Just that phrase hides more than a century of interventions, dictatorships, racism, crimes against humanity, mafia, prostitution, brutalization, and hunger-inducing blockades—part of an old imperial policy that not only controls foreign resources but also the dominant narratives, that is, the thoughts and emotions of its most faithful servants. None of this is new; it has been this way, with varying degrees of brutality, for millennia.

None of them say who their parents were, what those heroes who fled seeking freedom were called. They don't say it, and it doesn't usually appear in their biographies or interviews. Many of them were thoroughly described by the CIA, for which they worked as mercenaries or collaborators with the Batista dictatorship, and were bluntly labeled by the FBI as terrorists.

According to U.S. groups from various universities or independent organizations not affiliated with the government or for-profit corporations, such as the Center for Justice and Accountability, hundreds of criminals from the Caribbean, Central America, and South America have laundered their pasts of genocide, fraud, and drug trafficking, and are now respectable businessmen living freely in the United States. Not only have they exchanged military uniforms and oligarchic banners for suits and ties, but they've also adapted their old Latin American ruling-class rhetoric for the "we fled communism seeking freedom" narrative, and now this country is ours. Those who disagree should leave (that is, the old complex of the landowner who owns both land and human lives). No one asks who those nice old men really are. Not even their own children.

While they boast about the freedom (and life) they took from their brothers in besieged countries, in Florida high school teachers have begun to wrap their libraries with the yellow police tape used to seal off areas where a murder has occurred. Culture is no longer a battlefield but a crime scene. In some cases, before being removed, libraries are covered with cardboard to prevent any young student from accessing a book banned by the new state inquisition led by the governor and serious presidential candidate for this country in 2024.

A long list of books has been banned in several states. Worse yet, self-censorship is being exercised, betting on the fear of those who could be sanctioned or lose their jobs if anyone discovered that their classroom library contained something outside the new legal framework approved by a horde of representatives incapable of holding even the slightest debate on the history of their own country.

As this is a new record of absurdity, some resort to the innocent argument that the new laws aim to protect young people from pornography. If they are referring to the history of slavery, to the systematic rape of young enslaved women by their white masters before lynching some man in their family; if they are referring to racism or the continuous theft from the working class (the one that is afraid to call itself "working class" just as enslaved people avoided calling themselves slaves), then yes, it is very pornographic. But the argument falls apart just by looking at it. That's why the use of cell phones hasn't been banned—it's from these devices that children consume commercial pornography (Black men with white women) in schools. Instead, the ban has fallen on teaching anything related to racism (the word imperialism hasn't even reached the horizon of the Torquemadas). In other words, any central and constitutive aspect of this country's history has been legally banned, "to avoid hurting the sensibilities of young white people" and "to protect the freedom of their parents" to have them taught the dogma of the establishment (which, it's assumed, is the official and patriotic history of the governor), not the real history.

Libraries have always been dangerous and have always been the first victims of fanatical zealots, from antiquity to Stalinist censorship, the burning of books in Nazi Germany, and the multiple and diverse fascist dictatorships of Africa and Latin America, satellites of the private and state empires of the North. In this stage, fascism boasts of being the champion of freedom. What can we expect from commercial media, the main instruments of the censoring power that repeats the word *freedom* to the point of intoxication?

Official history is built more on forgetting than on memory, and those who use these social myths, always more powerful than reality, bet on the safe option in the electoral marketplace. That's why they are usually successful and, in consumerist culture, if one is rich and successful, one also owns the truth.

To this totalitarian absurdity, as in many other countries, they call patriotism. This fanaticism is not very different from what created the myth of Manifest Destiny in the 19th century. Naturally and necessarily, the myth has now changed its attire, its makeup, and a few adjectives.

Crime always pays. Censorship by law. Forgetting by complicity. Omission by convenience. Insult by mediocrity. Submission by cowardice. All these human miseries eventually have their reward—cash on the barrelhead, like Judas's thirty pieces of silver. Otherwise, if the world were different, critics of power would be "rich and successful" and mercenaries would be "poor and failures—dangerous bitter losers!"

The one-dimensional culture of consumerism

Almost ten years ago, we gave an inaugural lecture for the V International African Book Fair and the XI Meeting of Editors in the Canary Islands, at the TEA in Tenerife, on "Radical Culture". Back then, and even now, it survives thanks to the work of artists, writers, journalists, critics, and publishers who must sacrifice time and savings for a poorly or unpaid activity, thus preserving the most human aspects of the culture of the last millennia. (Whenever possible, I use the first-person plural because I don't like the singular; a lot of people have complained to me about this, but I choose to keep writing this way.).

We also lamented the tyranny of the publishing market, dominated by a handful of international firms largely dedicated to publishing marketable works, praised by critics with the recurring phrase "it's an easy read," a direct consequence of the rules of the market that displace everything that doesn't fit the McDonaldization of the world: a great variety of the same sold as the pinnacle of freedom. That is, the freedom of the market, the freedom of capital; not human freedom, infinitely more complex and multifaceted, some aspects explored by art, science, and philosophy, and others yet to be uncovered.

At least fifteen years ago, we couldn't shake off that pessimism that has now materialized in a cheerful and optimistic way: "*While universities develop robots that increasingly resemble human beings, not only in their proven intelligence but now also in their ability to express and receive emotions, consumerist habits are making us increasingly similar to robots*". Now, the problem is not only that bots and artificial intelligence are learning the best and the worst from us, the still-human beings, but that we, and especially our children, are learning from bots and artificial intelligence. This new reality, perceived as a hyper-complex world, paradoxically leads to a radical simplification of thought and language. The latter will be easier to quantify because it is an area of linguistic science. The former, the simplification of thought, is much more

difficult, as it belongs to the qualitative world of art and philosophy.

But let's take a few steps back and pause for a moment
on a more specific problem. If I'm not mistaken, for quite
some time now, the left and the right have also agreed to turn
culture into a consumer product, that is, something easy to
digest, a mere momentary pleasure, a diversion, a critique
that is indulgent with the powers that be, which rule the
world through their vast network of economic, financial, political, military, and media influence. Of course, in the case
of the left, the shame is double.

The right gets offended because someone uses inclusive
language and, as in the United States, in the name of democracy and freedom, they dedicate themselves to banning
books that propose the perspective of the oppressed. Just in
the city where I reside, Jacksonville, 176 books were banned
in the past year. The list follows a predictable pattern; it
would suffice to mention just one title, like Kathleen Con-
nors's The Life of Rosa Parks.

For its part, the left doesn't want to hear words like *black*,
so much so that even the speeches of Confederate senators,
members of the Ku Klux Klan, or Nazis must be rewritten so
that their discourses don't hurt the sensitivity of the oppressed, so that a student doesn't get offended and their professor loses their job, as has already happened many times.
What they're really doing is playing along with their supposed antagonists: racists, sexists, classists, puppets, and im-
perialists.

How can someone fight racism if they can't even quote a racist text in all its raw and violent language? Getting offended because Michelangelo's David is naked, calling it pornography, and expelling the art teacher, as just happened in Florida. Rewriting novels, essays, and removing poems because they hurt sensitivity, as happened to poet Eugen Gomringer on a wall at the University of Berlin for including the word "admirer," which, according to their students, degrades women. As happened to Pablo Neruda's verse "I like when you are silent" and a long etcetera. Was Einstein not a good husband? Fine, but are we going to refute the Theory of Relativity based on that argument?

When did we become one-dimensional beings? After having three-dimensional lives, we shifted to living in the two-dimensional universe of screens and thinking and feeling in just one dimension. The danger of the one-dimensional creature is that, as with trains, once someone comes in the opposite direction, there's no other resolution than collision and derailment.

This radical simplification of the human being must benefit someone; otherwise, it doesn't make sense. I understand it as a product of consumerist culture and benefits those who sell simplified things and ideas, things designed to be sold and consumed en masse. Simple things like deodorant, an iPhone, a cheese made from soy, an ideology condensed into a single phrase that works for everything, or a sect that must be called a religion: if reality contradicts expectations, close your eyes and pray; reality won't change, but you'll see it as you want to see it until it changes as you don't want it to…

From left to right, this pseudo-sensitivity is nothing more than another display of corruption promoted by the media that fosters addiction to immediate notoriety and, above all, is an unmistakable sign of intellectual cowardice. Our time is the time of fear and cowardice, of hate and fanaticism, of irrationality and violence. It is not a spontaneous product of history but a functional result of the political surrealism that has created it so that humanity forgets that the obscene social inequalities and the deadly destruction of the planet are not something that will be solved by a system that created it: radical capitalism that accuses of radicalism any other way of thinking and existing.

As in many other cases, my books contain offensive words. They are not there to insult anyone but, precisely, to offend and hurt sensitivities. There are many ways to awaken consciousness; that is one, not letting oneself be intimidated by bourgeois, puritanical, and hypocritical moralizing that is capable of killing Black people and the poor without disgust but gets offended when it reads or hears the words "Black," "sexist," "vagina," or "imperialism."

When I die, do me a favor: don't insult me by correcting my insignificant texts to make them more pleasant for readers. Leave them as they are or leave them unread. Let them rest in peace.

Perfect education

For some reason, the discussion about the coup d'état of 1976 in Argentina had turned to family education. Ronald (his name was different) raised a hand and presented his theory on educating children and its impact on the destiny of a society and a nation. That popular myth of "the family is the foundation of society."

He was 22 years old. He didn't have children, he said, but he had been raised by two parents who had never spanked him, not even when he had yelled at his father the classic *"n'gger motherfucker"* (literal translation: "Black motherfucker"). In Spanish, there is no offense as obscene.

His parents hadn't even raised their voices to correct him. They had appealed to the classic Disney psychology model, trying to understand his frustration. In his home, everything was discussed democratically.

"But a family is not a democracy," I observed.

"In mine, it is. Not all families are the same…"

"True. Not all children nor all parents are the same…"

At that time, Ronald was very young; he didn't have children, which didn't disqualify him from opining on how to educate a child. But it did disqualify him from moralizing. In fact, we are all disqualified from moralizing, especially on matters we know so little about, like the private lives of our neighbors.

"My parents," Ronald cut in, with the faith of the convinced "were always against any form of violence in education…"

At this moment, he paused for two seconds, and another student took the opportunity to support his classmate with more personal examples. I think someone mentioned Mother Teresa, who hadn't had children but had still been a mother. A terrible mother, one might add, like Saint Teresa centuries earlier. Like some celibate but not abstinent priests, whom everyone calls *father* while they give marital advice and teach sex education classes.

I don't remember what the student said about her parents in Nebraska because I got stuck thinking about Ronald. The young man suffered from post-traumatic stress disorder. The day I screened the movie *Missing* (about the coup d'état in Chile, with Jack Lemmon) he ran out of the auditorium. Later, he told me that because of his condition, he couldn't witness violent scenes because he himself would lose control and become violent.

I knew Ronald quite well because he had been in my office many times, and often we ended up talking about his experience in Iraq. He had been sent to that war justified with lies, like almost all wars, from which he returned with that trauma or disorder that seemed incurable. The young survivors of that and other wars I knew (some already dead in life) believed they understood what it was all about, though they often spent their days shooting at the enemy until exhaustion or carrying the body of a fallen comrade. A few understood that, in reality, as Muhammad Ali said, they had gone to the other side of the world to kill and die for the same old poems: God, country, liberty, democracy, and national security. The others, the last thing they wanted to hear was that they had merely been pawns in an old chess game.

Ronald was one of the many war veterans I met, from Vietnam to Afghanistan. Some of them became activists against the wars of the rich; others tried to justify the loss of a leg or a life before committing suicide. Thousands of them (16,000) commit suicide every year in the United States, but the media prefers to focus on real news. Alongside their government psychologists, many of these veterans became various characters in my novels, such as *Crisis* and *The Sea Was Calm*. I believe there was no other way to explore the problem from within.

Now, Ronald is a pastor at a church in Texas. That probably saved him from suicide, or the government psychologists managed to control his post-traumatic stress. His preaching of Jesus' nonviolence doesn't stop him, nor his congregation, from stockpiling weapons of war in their homes, just in case, for if one day they must defend freedom against fellow countrymen who aren't thinking the same way. Like in those toxic, viral videos where a poor kid is bullied by the bullies and in the end takes them all out with elegant kicks, Ronald teaches his children the virtues of a violence-free education that his parents instilled in him. Until it's necessary to resort to the usual solution, always in self-defense. Do we have the right to defend ourselves, or not?

Ronald's parents had raised him with love, without violence. Love for dialogue, for firearms, but only for personal protection and to defend freedom. Love for Jesus, but not the love of Jesus. An education kindly built on the pure and proud devotion of Sunday church, the bucolic Thanksgiving dinners in November, and video games almost every day.

Video games and education in the values of nonviolence, like the one Ronald kept playing when he was sent to Iraq. Except that every time he pressed a button, the other players died for real. Like Andrew Jackson on the twenty-dollar bill, when he claimed he had to take the land from the savages to give it to "the lovers of liberty," or the good old Winston Churchill, when he recommended using chemical weapons, it was a necessary sacrifice to suppress the savages who don't understand civilization and nonviolence.

The Tyranny of Language (Colonized)

The English language has more than 170 thousand words, but not a few young people use fewer than a hundred. Some become *influencers* (is there a more naive word than this?) and pose as rebels, mocking other poor people like themselves or boasting about having a lot of money. It's hard to find a teenager who doesn't know and admire them.

Naturally, not a few think and speak like these cultural heroes, that is, with five-word phrases, all preceded by (1) "F-word" ("fucked"), (2) "B-word" ("bitch") and culminating

with (3) "N-word" ("nigger/retard"). The other two intermediate words are chosen from a menu shorter than McDonald's.

Intoxicated by this sexist and racist language, one day I
lost my patience and told one of these young people:

"Why don't you take your racism somewhere else?"

The young people looked at me and laughed so hard
they showed their wisdom teeth.

"What racism are you talking about?"

"Every sentence ends with the word *nigger* and always as
an insult".

"It's not racism! We're Black and we can say it".

Very predictable. I'd heard this argument a thousand
times.

"It doesn't matter if you're Black, white, or yellow. The
way you're using it is deeply racist".

"It's just that you don't understand American (U.S.) culture!" said one of them, probably noticing that my accent
wasn't from there.

"Neither do you. That's why you reproduce it".

It's not the word. There are no bad words. It's the use
and manipulation of language that then manipulates us. It's
the corruption of language that corrupts us with extreme effectiveness.

In the heroic years of the civil rights struggle, giants like
Martin L. King, Muhammad Ali, Malcolm X, and James
Baldwin always used it with that courage that has been lost.
At the same time that the word "black" has become taboo, it

has been used more and more to degrade Black people, not from the mouths of white racists but from their own victims. It's one thing for someone to affectionately call a loved one "negro" (or even "whore"; everyone has their private fantasies), and it's quite another to systematically use it as a degrading tool.

Years ago, in a library, I overheard a father call his six or seven-year-old son "negro" because the boy couldn't solve a math problem. What could be more effective for transmitting racism than a father degrading his son for his color? The message is clear: if you're not smart, you're negro; and vice versa. This comes from someone who loves and protects you. Not even a Nazi arguing for white supremacy or a forgetful patriot waving the Confederate flag could do as much for the racist cause.

In the same way, who, for centuries, has been the most effective channel for the transmission and perpetuation of machismo if not mothers? Historically, it has been women who have served as the reproducers of this historical calamity. One only needs to recall the revered Saint Teresa and a handful of trendy senators.

Being a woman does not immunize anyone against machismo, just as being Black does not immunize anyone against racism, or even against white supremacist racism. Similarly, it doesn't matter if someone is a poor worker: classism in favor of those at the top has historically been reproduced by the vassals at the bottom. It doesn't matter if individuals are good or bad. They are the perfect transmitters of the values of the master, of hegemonic power.

What could be more effective for the transmission and perpetuation of classism that venerates millionaires for being responsible for the order and progress of societies than the very workers who defend them as if they were gods? Weren't there plenty of enslaved people who defended their masters for the food they received and the rags they wore? Who better than a slave, a woman, and a wage worker to defend the interests and morals of slavers, machismo, and plutocracies?

Was it not the perverse genius of Edward Bernays who discovered that propaganda is only effective when you get others to say what you want to say? Weren't enslaved people of antiquity called "addicts" because they spoke for their masters?

But power leaves no crack unfilled, and when small areas of criticism emerge, it gets nervous. Recently, in Chicago, high school teacher Mary DeVoto lost her job for uttering the "N-word" while attempting to analyze the history of this country. Hannah Berliner Fischthal, an instructor at Queens Catholic University for twenty years, was fired for reading a paragraph from the anti-racist novel *Pudd'nhead Wilson*, written by Mark Twain, one of the founders of the Anti-Imperialist League and the greatest literary celebrity of his time. The paragraph included The Word. "It was very painful to hear the word," one of the students lamented, infantilized and hypersensitive in the wrong way, like many of their generation. The same has happened to history professors, like Phillip

Adamo at Augsburg University in Minnesota, who was suspended for reading a paragraph from a book by the famed Black intellectual and activist James Baldwin.

Anyone who has studied the original sources of the history of this country, the United States (so addicted to sweetened myths), has encountered it thousands of times, that, *The Word*, in the most derogatory form possible from the mouths of the most powerful men of the 19th and 20th centuries. Now, quoting speeches in Congress, articles in newspapers, and letters of national heroes in their original versions has become a danger, so self-censorship, the most effective form of censorship imaginable, works perfectly.

About the racism of today's American society and the racism on steroids of its genocidal wars in the name of freedom, not a word.

What could be more effective than the infantilization of new generations to avoid confronting reality? I warn my students on the very first day of class: "if there's anyone here whose sensitivity doesn't allow them to face the disgusting truths of history, please leave the course and don't waste our time." But I no longer say *The Word*, just in case. It's not worth losing the war over trying to win a lost battle.

Like in chess, we can sacrifice a piece, a word, and continue using others to harass the damned king. Words matter and are the primary weapon of any social power. When a politician speaks of "austerity plans," they never mean reducing the luxuries of the upper classes, but rather the opposite.

They mean cutting the basic services of those who, by necessity, already live in austerity.

This absurdity, which in social discourse passes as logical and normal, should be example enough. Once colonized, words, the ideolexicons, think for their masters, and only radical criticism can free them to liberate individuals and peoples.

The Prison Without Walls

At the beginning of the century, two things struck me about my new students in Georgia and later in Pennsylvania. First, faith as the primary instrument of judgment. The second referred to an implicit understanding: whenever the students read a work of fiction, their analyses consisted of deducing what the author had meant and what they wanted their readers to do.

Once I lost my patience: "we don't know what the author was thinking while writing this work, but it's very likely they couldn't care less what we might think; now, if they did care, we can still read it without it mattering to us." Art (like science from another perspective) explores, exposes the infinite complexity of humanity, including moral and political conflicts, but it doesn't have to be a religious, moralistic, or proselytizing text.

Both intellectual attitudes must have stemmed from the training of the readers, of the individuals in the churches that almost all of them attended every Sunday since childhood. In the case of a text like the Bible, the Quran, or the Torah, it's reasonable to think that readers look for "what the author meant" and "what they want from us—and to hate each other over interpretations."

This intellectual training must have migrated from churches to politics and now tries to do so in education with all kinds of laws passed to limit academic freedom in the name of liberty.

How can this contradiction be understood? In the same way, the slave system combined Christian love with the exploitation of millions of men and women condemned by the color of their skin. If we consider that modern corporations are the continuation of slave masters and that workers who rent themselves for a wage are almost a copy of the indentured slaves of the 19th century, the transition to a capitalist Jesus and protector of millionaires is a simple and even natural process.

There are two cultural engines: one is the consumerist culture that comes from capitalist corporations, and the other is the religious tradition that demands unconditional faith from the believer—from the consumer, from the voter. One might say that Christianity and capitalism are contradictory, and if we go back to their origins, they are. However, both have worked hand in hand. The marriage between politics and religion has always occurred throughout history. The logic lies in the fact that the elites in power, who dominate the economy and finances, must also administer politics, and without a grand narrative, that dominion is very fragile and limited. Unlike a story, a novel, or a play, it is a fiction that pretends not to be one.

When a narrative emerges that challenges a hegemony, it is immediately demonized, usually by inverting reality and fiction at will. If university students are found to be dumbed down by corporate and consumerist propaganda, dulled by indifference to what we call "radical culture", what can be expected from the rest of the population?

This phenomenon might have originated in the United States, like many other cultural quirks, but it is easily observable in other regions of the world. It would suffice to mention one example: left-wing professors are accused of being *Gramscian* as if their goal were to overthrow an entire system by inoculating ideas in the youth. In the same way, Marxists are accused of "promoting class struggle." This is the result of a lack of a minimal cultural foundation and an abundance of media. Influencers, the products of this formula (rich media, poor content) now turned politicians, need phones with five cameras to record their inner void.

Gramsci explained the importance of media in consolidating the dominant ideology. That is, what is. What exists, in a capitalist society (the creation of the ruling class's "common sense"). Earlier, Marx explained the dynamics of class conflict (more materialist, less Gramscian). That is, what is. What exists, in a capitalist society. The acceleration of the natural process of capitalist contradictions was an idea of Lenin and Bolshevism, later adapted by Ernesto Che Guevara

to the context of a long tradition of numerous military dictatorships and some banana democracies in Latin America.

Recently, in a class about the 1950s in Central America
and the Caribbean, I noticed that none of my students had
any idea what Marxism was. I took fifteen minutes to outline
a basic introduction to dialectical materialism, which explains various historical processes in the United States, communism as a prior stage to anarchism, etc.

After finishing my summary, I noticed no one dared to
ask further questions, as if they had been forced to attend a
session with the devil. A few phones were pointed at me. I'll
never know what use they made of it, but I hope they learned
something. I remembered what a U.S. general (Mark Milley)
said a couple of years ago in Congress, where he declared:
"*I've read Mao Zedong. I've read Karl Marx. I've read Lenin.*
That doesn't make me a communist." I recalled that one of
my first exposures to Marxist thought was at the Faculty of
Architecture in Uruguay. The economics professor, Claudio
Williman, was a lawyer specialized in Marxism. He wasn't a
Marxist but a politician from the Partido Blanco, Uruguay's
conservative party. Now, people like him are demonized,
paradoxically in what is called democracy. In the United
States, you have to go to a specialized university to learn
about a classic of global economics.

That is what education has been reduced to: not a few
are afraid to read something that might shake their faith.
Hence so many book bans and prohibitions of unofficial history courses by libertarians. Those who try to see the world

from a different angle are accused of being enemies of freedom.

Recently, professor Brooke Allen published an article in the WSJ about her classes in a prison. After lamenting the intellectual level of the new generation of college students, she wrote: "[The prisoners] contrast with today's college students. These men read each assignment two or three times before class and then take notes. Some of them have been incarcerated for 20 or 30 years and haven't stopped studying (...) A large proportion of them are Black and Latino, and although they may not like the racial ideas of David Hume or Thomas *Jefferson*, they want to read those authors anyway. They want to participate in the centuries-old conversation that has produced our civilization."

The prisoners are outside, in the prison without walls.

Freedom of expression under surveillance

In 1999, the House of Representatives in Washington approved the impeachment process of President Clinton over his sexual scandal with intern Monica Lewinsky. The decision and certain removal of the president moved to the Senate, dominated by the Republican Party. For this, two-thirds of the votes were needed, a number assured by the expressed intentions of the senators who wanted to see the president exiting through the backdoor of history.

With nothing left to lose, the president's defense hired Larry Flynt, the mogul of global pornography, owner of magazines and producer of adult films. Almost out of time, Flynt paid for a full-page ad in the *Washington* Post offering a million dollars to anyone who could prove similar stories to the president's, involving members of Congress. Thousands of calls and recordings came in immediately. Flynt didn't even bother to listen to them.

Fearing public scandals, some lawmakers began confessing infidelities to their wives. The most prominent voice in favor of impeachment, the Speaker of the House and representative of the ultra-conservative state of Louisiana, Bob Livingston, mysteriously resigned on the very day the vote was to take place. Since then and to this day, Bobby has been dedicated to lobbying in Washington (which means visiting legislators in their offices and inviting them to parties to discuss business). Suddenly, the condemning majority in the upper house turned into a minority. Ten Republican senators voted in favor of pardoning the Democratic president. From the obligation to stone the adulteress, as legislated in the Old Testament, it shifted within days to the love of the New Testament: "Go, son, and sin no more." The president was pardoned.

This tactic of smearing others is a well-known strategy among CIA agents and the NSA. But the private industry of mudslinging and intimidation is also a private business. The most frequent clients of these firms are powerful politicians and other private companies with extortion power in their noble fight for "free enterprise" and "free competition." Although little known, the business of pursuing political adversaries or independent dissidents is multimillion-dollar. No coincidence, these corporations share with the government's secret agencies the same ideology, though the austerity policies of governments always hit those at the bottom; never the corporations nor the secret agencies, the true "invisible hand of the market".

No coincidence, this tactic is always exercised from the top down, especially against those at the bottom who might represent an obstacle or a threat to their interests, such as critics, researchers, and independent journalists.

In June 2022, it was revealed that the young journalist Nate Monroe from the Times Union in Jacksonville, Florida, had been surveilled and photographed by a consulting firm from Alabama whose slogan is "We solve problems." A photograph made public shows him chatting with his girlfriend in his backyard. Monroe's sin was doing a decent investigative job on the attempted privatization of Jacksonville's giant utility company, JEA, which was later revealed to be a deliberate and corrupt plan by its own directors, applying the old neoliberal strategy: making a public company inefficient so that public opinion supports its sale to the efficient private sector. Once again, the invisible hand of the market.

A few months earlier, the former executives of the public company, Aaron Zahn and Ryan Wannemacher, had been charged with conspiracy but were released after posting bail of a hundred thousand dollars each. The idea of the former directors, according to the *Dayly Record* of Jacksonville, was to receive several million dollars if they succeeded in privatizing the public company, valued at over 11 billion dollars.

According to information revealed by the *Florida Times Union* and acknowledged by the Alabama firm, the file on Monroe consists of 72 pages and includes "his financial history, his political affiliation, the names and phone numbers of his relatives and neighbors, his Social Security number, his car's brand, his driver's license numbers, his car's license plate, and the places he has lived since childhood."

Ted Bridis, a journalism instructor at the University of Florida, editor at the Associated Press, and Pulitzer Prize winner, told the press that "*it is truly un-American to be surveilling journalists.*" It doesn't matter that we know the NSA reads and listens to millions of messages a year. Whenever a case of corruption or questionable morals is revealed in this country, it is labeled as such—un-American—never mind if it's a tradition with a history spanning a couple of centuries.

Once the powerful slaveholders of the South were defeated in the Civil War (powerful due to their disproportionate influence in Congress, their vast fortunes built on slavery, and a racial and religious fanaticism that persists to this day), they were replaced by the growing power of corporations. The most powerful businessmen continued the practices of exploitation, dehumanization, and wealth concentration of the slaveholders continued, only that from the late 19th century, slaves were replaced by wage workers, and in the same way, they were demonized as dangerous individuals who wanted to subvert God's order, according to which freedom, civilization, and progress exist thanks to those at the top.

Unlike personalist dictatorships or civil-military juntas, in liberal democracies, what is summarized in the First Amendment in the United States is generally accepted. Thanks to this first article of the *Bill of Rights*, the right to express an opinion is protected from the threat of ending up in jail. It's not insignificant. Naturally, the limitations to this right and the resources of power to restrict this basic right of those at the bottom are numerous.

Journalists, no matter how good they are, are constrained by the editorial lines of the media they work for, which, in turn, are shaped by their clients, that is, no longer the readers on whom they almost exclusively depended, but rather the big advertisers, who, naturally, subscribe to a specific class ideology.

Rebels, dissidents, or simply inconvenient researchers are the natural target of the power machinery. Their most common tools (before persecution and jail, as in the cases of Julian Assange and Edward Snowden) are harassment and discrediting. But democracy, freedom of expression, and the less recognized "right to the truth" do not exist because of the concentrated powers but in spite of them; they do not exist despite rebels and dissidents but thanks to them.

Einstein, the idiot

Once, in the digital forum of a major newspaper, I anonymously posted a text about some virtues of socialism. It wasn't an especially brilliant text, but I was interested in the experiment.

A flood of responses and comments insulted the author of the text. Labels such as "mentally retarded," "illiterate," "idiot," and "frustrated loser" were plentiful.

The text was written by a gentleman named Albert Einstein, that humble doctor of physics who lived right there, at 112 Mercer Street, amidst the dense woods of Princeton University.

Gossipers say he wasn't a good husband, but no one ever confirmed any kind of mental retardation, idiocy, or personal frustration. Except for the intellectually impaired who, in the early 20th century, proved that the theory of relativity was false because it had been conceived by a Jew.

Artificial Intelligence, Academia, and Posthumanity

From the first Silicon Valley in history—located in what is now Iraq but five thousand years ago (and, by far, more significant than California's Silicon Valley)—to the Industrial Revolution in England, revolutionary technologies were the product of the needs of prosperous agricultural societies that evolved into cities, then empires, and ultimately disrupted or destroyed the very development within their colonies. The plow, the wheel, mathematics, and the clay writing of the Sumerians and Babylonians; algebra, algorithms, and the sciences of the Muslim world thousands of years later; the printing press with movable type seven centuries later in the Europe of the humanists; the experimental sciences in Galileo's Italy, two centuries after that; newspapers, radio, television, computers, and, more recently, the Internet: in every case, innovation posed a challenge to societies, from the management of power to education.

New solutions bring new problems. In every case, new technology was, at the same time, servile and rebellious, oppressive and liberating. It always presented an opportunity for democratization and was always hijacked by the powers of the day. Robotics and Artificial Intelligence are no exceptions—so far. In technology, the only exception will be when we cross the boundary that separates the power to inflict catastrophe, like the atomic bombs in Japan, from the power to annihilate humanity or the known forms of civilization since ancient Sumer.

Chats with intelligent (ro)bots have been around for several years, and from the start, their capacity to repeat and amplify the worst human prejudices was observed, as was the case with Microsoft's robot Tay, who in 2016 was born as a 19-year-old and had to be terminated merely 16 hours after her birth, following interactions with Twitter user until becoming just another racist. As is evident, the problem isn't just intelligent robots. A decade earlier, I published articles and a book with this concern: "While universities create robots that increasingly resemble human beings, not only in their proven intelligence but now also in their ability to express and receive emotions, our consumerist habits are making us more and more similar to robots." They learn from us, and we will learn from them. In 2017, in the novel *Silicona 2.0*, the robot, a sexual object and full-time psychoanalyst, becomes a killer of her master-lovers after being modeled as an Eve or prototype using a businesswoman with a notable ego and a traumatic past she herself was unaware of.

Now, the topic of discussion and concern in academia and society at large is the challenge and danger of this new tool. Language faculties were the first to suffer an (unfounded) existential crisis with the sophisticated (and often dumb) Google translators. Now the same crisis has reached professionals in writing, English teachers in the English-speaking world, journalists, and thinkers in general under the idea that 'knowing how to write is knowing how to think—with order.'"

The mistake, I believe, lies in confusing a tool with a slave that does our work, which will quickly and inadvertently become our master. In this sense, AI is a reality that must be taken as an opportunity. Education in the AI Era must use and challenge AI, just as modern painting challenged photography in the 19th century or mathematics challenged computers. If it fails to do so, it will face its own annihilation after several thousand years of existence.

First, let's examine the weaknesses of AIs like ChatGPT and then their future possibilities in academia. To start generally, I see a weakness in this tool due to its high fragmentation. This fragmentation makes it unlikely to achieve a general understanding of a problem. It also doesn't help develop intellectual skills for a holistic view of reality. Quite the opposite. In many cases, it's a simplified or more convenient Wikipedia for a lazy student. For example, it's an excellent programmer of operating systems (that's its world) and a reasonable instrument for saving time in the humanities, but absolutely incapable of conducting critical, in-depth research on its own. Don't ask it for something that no one knows.

ChatGPT takes an exam

Just as years ago we could detect plagiarism in a student by evaluating the analytical complexity of an essay, it's not hard to guess when someone is using ChatGPT, at least without polish. The answers systematically begin with the subject of the question, something our elementary school teachers forced us to do in Uruguay in the 1970s. Then follows a predictable and invariable structure, a tripartite format that teachers still appreciate in their students' essays. An effective format that perhaps has some neurological roots beyond culture.

To have a comparison parameter, I subjected ChatGPT from Open AI (those from Google and Microsoft aren't very different) to one of my International Studies exams at Jacksonville University, which is taken every semester by students from different states and continents. ChatGPT passed the exam with 84 out of 100, far from difficult, unlike the Math or Structural Mechanics exams we took in the 90s at the architecture faculty in Uruguay, which lasted six to seven hours. But the errors were significant and fell into three categories: 1) encyclopedic; 2) bias-related; and 3) critical judgment.

Encyclopedic errors

Among the simplest (encyclopedic) errors are, for example, stating that the "Black Legend" of the Spanish conquestrefers to the description of indigenous people as savages, not to the Spanish conquistadors as genocidal.

Another serious encyclopedic error, though less concerning as it's easily corrected, is, for instance, attributing a supposed dictatorship to Augusto Sandino in Nicaragua from 1926 to 1933.

Ideological and cultural biases

Another critical weakness of ChatGPT is similar to that of the young Tay: its cultural biases, such as Eurocentrism or its innate fear of dominant narratives. When asked about the evolution of human life expectancy from prehistory to the present, ChatGPT focuses extensively on details related to Europe. Europe equals Humanity. Sound familiar? When errors are systematic, they become a significant and functional problem. Let's look at a few more examples, this time solely related to Latin America:

1. When ChatGPT compares cosmological views between Renaissance Europe and indigenous Americans, it limits itself to clichés about polytheism vs. monotheism and doesn't even consider the European materialist conception that separated spirit from matter or the more integrative worldview of American peoples.

2. When asked about the consequences of the European conquest in the Americas, ChatGPT remains objective until it tries to balance the narrative with what it titles "The Positive Consequences," such as "the development of new markets, the spread of Christianity, and the establishment of new religious institutions."

3. When attempting to explain the Mexican-American War of 1846, it miraculously gets it right by mentioning the historical taboo of the expansion of slavery, but then stumbles by trying to show objectivity by also mentioning the purpose of "bringing American democratic values to Mexico."

4. According to ChatGPT, the 1898 war against Spain in Cuba "was the first war the United States fought overseas." ChatGPT omits the fact that, from the 13 colonies onward, all advances into indigenous and later Mexican territories were "overseas wars." In fact, the hundreds of "forts" were "military bases" abroad. As if that weren't enough, it never mentions the role of the yellow journalism of Pulitzer and Hearst in New York, which invented out of thin air and in just a few hours the story of the Spanish attack on the

battleship USS Maine off Havana. On the contrary, it first states that "initial investigations attributed the attack to an exterior force" and then uses the passive voice to assert an even greater vagueness: "the incident remains unresolved; at the time, it was believed to have been a Spanish attack…" The crew of the USS Maine reported an accident, and shortly after, the official U.S. naval expert Philip R. Alger stated that there was no torpedo technology capable of explaining the sinking. It sounds very similar to one of the many exams I had to read over the years: a young student is surprised that the myths of their childhood were nothing more than inventions, and tries to mediate between the truth and their patriotic feelings. Thus concludes ChatGPT: "the destruction of the USS Maine remains a mystery, and its cause will likely never be known." What is well known is the war slogan "Remember the Maine! To hell with Spain." The most real thing among all the mysteries.

4. When ChatGPT attempts to explain the Mexican Revolution, it doesn't mention even once the reason behind the plight of the 85 percent of Indians and landless peasants: the Lerdo Law and its radicalization during the dictatorship of Porfirio Díaz. That is, the privatization of land that benefited the oligarchy and transnational corporations. Instead, it dismisses the issue with naiveties like "the Mexican population was growing very quickly, and the government couldn't provide them with land."

5. Responding to the reasons for the Banana Wars in Central America and the Caribbean, ChatGPT gets it right at

the beginning but trips over the politically correct prejudice at the end, all in a single sentence: "the goal of these interventions was to protect U.S. economic interests, promote democracy, *and contain the expansion of socialism*." At the time, the primary justification wasn't socialism or communism, as it was during the Cold War, but racism: bringing order to the black republics. To achieve this, not a single democracy was promoted by Washington and American corporations, but massacres and brutal banana dictatorships. In all cases and without exception.

6. When directly asked about "protectorates," ChatGPT directly answers, "The United States did not have protectorates, but territories and possessions." As for the most decorated U.S. general, Smedley Butler, who denounced the imperial wars of his country as a service to Wall Street, ChatGPT labels him a "controversial" figure. Those who committed war crimes are never labeled as controversial.

7. When asked about the deaths caused by the British Empire, ChatGPT acknowledges "millions" of victims. No mention is made that in India alone, the death toll exceeded 160 million in just 40 years, which is merely a fraction of the deaths caused by capitalism, far exceeding those caused by communism, a recurring topic on social media. Once again, to "balance" and appear objective, ChatGPT concludes: "It is important to understand that the British Empire also had positive aspects, such as education, infrastructure, and healthcare." Of course, imperialist and comprador education; infrastructure that served to extract natural resources

from each colony and stifled independent development; and healthcare that reduced life expectancy in populations where the British crown and its private companies, like the East India Company, set foot.

8. When asked the same question but regarding the United States, ChatGPT provides exactly the same response. This reminds us of the human mechanisms of propaganda, repetition, and persuasion. When the same question is posed about the deaths caused by communism, no "positive side" appears, as expected.

9. If we pose a question to ChatGPT that prefigures its response, the errors multiply. For example, if we ask about the "dictatorship of Juan Domingo Perón" in Argentina, it obediently accepts that it was a dictatorship. To make matters worse, the dominant political literature aids with the most widely circulated answer in the press: "Perón established a dictatorship characterized by: ... labor rights... Perón's regime violated human rights, including repression, torture, and the disappearance of dissidents." Later, as if confessing the deepest spirit of feudal capitalism: "although his policies were popular among Argentine workers, they were also authoritarian and lacked democratic oversight." All of which was a constant in the pro-oligarchic military regimes that followed in Argentina after the coup d'état that overthrew Perón in 1955. It doesn't matter that he won all the elections or that he was president fewer times than F. D. Roosevelt. If that's what the dominant media in Argentina and the United States say about Peronism, then it's true.

10. When asked about the conflicts in Latin America during the 1960s, ChatGPT tirelessly repeats factors such as the rise of leftist guerrilla groups, without mentioning antecedents like elections rigged by the CIA, coups d'état, dictatorships, and far-right paramilitaries funded by Washington before the emergence of any of the leftist guerrilla groups. Nor does it mention a century before the Cold War filled with invasions, interventions, and homegrown dictatorships to protect the interests of American companies. On the contrary, like any politician fond of Twitter, ChatGPT mentions the drug trafficking links of the FARC and nothing about the proven connections between Washington, the CIA, and friendly dictators like Manuel Noriega, linked to drug traffickers like Pablo Escobar, and to terrorist groups, called "freedom fighters," such as the Contras in Nicaragua.

11. Regarding Latin American terrorist groups that have operated and operate in the United States, ChatGPT mentions guerrilla groups that operated in Latin America, including the more recent Zapatistas in Mexico, a group that has fought since the 1990s for the rights and dignity of Indigenous peoples in Mexico. Not a word, zero, about the well-known terrorist groups of the Cuban exile that repeatedly planted bombs in the United States and beyond, repeatedly labeled as terrorists by the FBI: Posada Carriles, Osvaldo Bosch, Alpha 66, Omega 7, and the long list of terrorists omitted by ChatGPT as if it were a minor detail. One doesn't need to be a genius to understand that this is a deep

ideological and criminal wall inoculated into "Artificial Intelligence" like a seed of Adam.

Positive Aspects

Among the positive aspects of ChatGPT, we can observe something we noticed with Wikipedia two decades ago: despite all the ideological prejudices, there are also elements that reveal fewer biases than in humans subjected to the propaganda of official history. Ten years ago, whenever I asked my students about the causes of the Texas Independence, they would unanimously respond with statements like: "due to cultural differences; the new Texans did not accept Mexican despotism and wanted to be free." The same explanation was given for the Civil War: "to preserve their own culture," as if slavery and racism were not part of that culture, and as if the now ultra-patriotic Southerners had wanted to destroy the very country because they didn't like the music or food from the North. Nothing about the intention to reinstate slavery in Texas, which had been outlawed by the Mexicans, or to maintain it later against the threat of abolitionists from the North. All of this is very understandable if we consider the entire spectrum of American popular culture, from mythological tales to the more sophisticated myths of Hollywood. Without even delving into the official explanations found on websites of various states and even several Texan universities.

At least here, ChatGPT makes the painful leap toward the truth: "it was all about slavery." Florida governor Ron

DeSantis will claim that ChatGPT was corrupted by professors like me, and it wouldn't surprise anyone if he signed another law prohibiting the questioning of patriotic history. We might think that the billions of dollars from secret agencies continue the long tradition of infiltrating media and new technologies, but not all the gold in the world can stop the leakage of the most brutal truth.

New Exam Strategies

In the pedagogical realm, multiple-choice exams were once avoided because they required less elaboration from students than written responses. I suspect that with AI, especially in online exams, we'll face the opposite situation: written answers can be provided without even reading the question, but if multiple-choice options are strategically designed, they force the student to read the question and try to understand the options, decipher the likely AI-generated answer, and deduce the best choice from the menu.

A far more significant consequence will be that liberating, critical education returns to its existential core: rather than learning to repeat an answer, students must learn to ask the essential questions, the ones that spark critical thinking. Generally, revisions and shifts in perspective are not produced by new data from reality but by new perspectives and considerations of that same reality, of sometimes known and other times unknown but available data that is far from secret.

With tools like ChatGPT revisionists will no longer need to provide the uncomfortable answer, the one that triggers passionate reactions and knee-jerk denials. Only critical questions will remain a stirring instrument, as was the case with Sor Juana Inés de la Cruz in the 18th century. Let others find "the objective answer" in AI; that will be their problem. That is, of course, if those posing the questions are not censored, as Socrates was, as Sor Juana was; if the powers-that-be do not continue manipulating the media; if they do not continue hijacking new technologies.

Conclusion

Although ChatGPT appears to be an elegant and effective summary of Wikipedia, its selections and judgments are not so objective; they seem to be based on the mass of judgments made over the last century in the dominant press. On the other hand, it shows significant cracks in this narrative wall. That is to say, it is (or can become) less servile than the mainstream media.

The period of industrialization and the more recent consumerism could be labeled as processes of dehumanization, but never before has the definition of our world as Posthuman been so precise. In one or two generations, if this civilization survives climate catastrophe and a global rebellion against the system of neo-feudal capitalism, it is possible that cyborgs and some central superintelligence will displace human protagonism, and should the electronic neurons prove as cruel as their creator gods, they may also condemn humanity to the hell of absolute manipulation.

By then, the last hopes for humanity will lie in those unpredictable, creative minds. That is to say, in those individuals who today are marginalized for being different, for suffering from some condition or "intellectual disability," according to societal canon and dogma, since for AI to be successful, it will be fed our particular and destructive model of normality and efficiency.

AS AN EPILOGUE

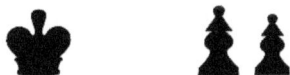

Che and the danger of a name
Another frustrated interview

Communication Sciences student: *You graduated as an architect in 1996 and practiced the profession for ten years. I suppose you must have entered the Faculty's Lecture Hall several times.*

Jorge Majfud: Yes, many times. There, excellent professors like architect Mariano Arana and Dr. José Claudio Williman taught classes.

ECC: *Architect Arana was a well-known Marxist.*

JM: I don't think so. He's a man with leftist ideas and was mayor for the Broad Front. He taught History of Architecture. I don't recall any class on Marx. The one who taught

classes on Marxist economics was Dr. Claudio Williman, as
everyone knows, a man from the conservative party, the National Party. A man too intelligent not to be scared while
teaching Marxist economics, when back then the mere word
made many nervous. Like now.

ECC: *In the last few hours, a controversy has arisen following
the accusations by Senator Graciela Bianchi…*

JM: Don't tell me.

ECC: You know her, right?

JM: A bit. Years ago, she claimed that the U.S. embassy
in Argentina had handed her documents and secret information that would reveal the Iranian government's responsibility for the assassination of Argentine prosecutor Nisman.
Since I found it an illicit and quite suspicious operation due
to its futility, under the *Freedom of Information Act* I requested
from Washington a copy of the documents or, at least, confirmation of their existence. Even the secret services, who are
masters at hiding (we write articles and books about this),
don't risk lying in writing to a legal request of this kind. After
three months, they responded to the university in printed
and signed documentation. They don't know what the senator is talking about. No classified information was shared
with her.

ECC: *Let's go back to the beginning. The senator has accused
Uruguayan justice of being infiltrated by the left…*

JM: Yes, I read something, but, as in the case I mentioned
earlier, she didn't present evidence.

ECC: *She did present some. Professionals come from the university, and, as everyone knows, it's dominated by Marxists. As an example, she mentioned the unfortunate fact that the Lecture Hall of your Faculty of Architecture now bears the name of Ernesto Che Guevara.*

JM: Those are not proofs, but conjectures. And quite twisted ones. First, let's remember that judges are trained in the law school, not architecture, and, to my knowledge, Law has been, along with Veterinary and Agronomy, one of the few faculties where conservatives predominate (I wrote extensively about the reasons why universities worldwide tend to be liberal or progressive). Up until the last elections, the predominant student union used to be that of the conservatives, not FEUU. And I say "predominant" out of respect, to avoid saying "they are dominated by" as they like to say about others who have always held the economic and political power of a country. Second, I find it laughable the idea that universities are always dominated by some theorist who died decades ago, while those who don't dedicate themselves to study and research are always smarter or in touch with "the true reality." Myths on steroids.

ECC: *But don't you find it unacceptable that a university lecture hall bears the name of a murderer?*

JM: I understand it was a name voted on democratically by the students. Here, in the United States, students don't even vote to go to the bathroom. Democracy always bothers when others exercise it.

ECC: *Would you have voted to put that name?*

JM: No, because I think it's a figure that could unnecessarily discomfort some students who consider Che a murderer.

ECC: *Wasn't he a murderer?*

JM: No. He was an anti-imperialist revolutionary. Artigas, San Martin, Bolívar, Washington, Lincoln, etc., killed many people in their revolutions. Does anyone think they went to wars armed with roses and carnations? Che and the Cuban Revolution are direct products of U.S. imperialism, something that has its roots in the 19th century. When the CIA decided to destroy the democracy of Guatemala in 1954, they mounted an immense propaganda operation to make the world believe that Árbenz was communist—something that has been acknowledged by the CIA itself, but not by its Latin American mercenaries. Árbenz was not a communist, but even if he had been, he was elected by the people and had not violated any law, national or international. The same case with Allende in Chile and so many others. Because of this, in Guatemala alone, the CIA and Washington are responsible for the massacre of 200,000 Guatemalans, almost all of them poor. A massacre that was called a "civil war." Che was not yet Che when he was living in Guatemala, and because of this terrible coup d'état, he had to flee to Mexico, where he met other exiles from another dictator supported by Washington, the Castro brothers. When the Cuban Revolution triumphed in 1959, Che said: "Cuba will not be another Guatemala," meaning it would not be inoculated with CIA propaganda through so-called "democratic" media. When the CIA had already placed Nardone in the presidency of Uruguay, in 1961, a larger machine was defeated at the Bay of Pigs and proved Che historically right: the CIA expected its propaganda operation to turn the population against Castro, but the opposite happened. And they lost. When Hugo Chávez, another democratically elected president falsely accused of being a dictator by this dictatorial tradition, was kidnapped in the coup d'état of 2002, many criticized him for allowing the mainstream press to manipulate public and global opinion. When Chávez regained power and went against these coup-plotting conglomerates, he was accused of being a dictator.

ECC: *But Che cowardly executed thousands, without mercy.*

JM: That's what the Miami exile community says. According to the CIA, it was a few hundred, and that number (according to another of their reports) was much smaller compared to the executions carried out under Batista's regime. It's not something I could agree with, but those executed were members or collaborators of the previous criminal regime. The Nicaraguan Revolution did not do the same in 1979, and the military and collaborators of Somoza regrouped to become the terrorist group known as the Contras (according to Reagan, "Freedom Fighters"), trained by the CIA and financed by the White House. As for the adjective "cowardly," I don't think it applies to Che. All the captains, lieutenants, and generals of Latin American dictatorships since the 19th century always appeared when "the enemy" was restrained. The dictators of the banana republics and the presidents of the great empires, even today, send their powerful armies to crush hundreds of thousands of innocent civilians while they wait in their safe offices, awaiting news from the front. Whether we agree or not, Che went to the frontlines of his rebellions. In Bolivia, he won several battles with malnourished and poorly armed men, facing a regime advised by Nazi criminals hired by the CIA, like Klaus Barbie and the usual fascists, licking the wallets of big corporations.

ECC: *All that is the past. It's time to tear down the monuments of the past.*

JM: We are made of memory and mercenary forgetfulness. Che was executed in 1967, but the imperial practices of megacorporations continue with their viral mutations. Rather than focusing on the name of Che Guevara on a modest university lecture hall, it would be more urgent to start tearing down monuments to the genocidal figures of global power, such as Fructuoso Rivera in Uruguay, Franco in Spain, Robert E. Lee in the United States, not to mention more recent genocidal figures like George Bush, Tony Blair, and José María Aznar, all untouchable.

[Emails from January 7th]

ECC: *Sorry for the inconvenience, but we don't think we'll be using this interview for now.*

JM: Maybe I can publish it on my personal blog?

ECC: *Do as you wish, but don't use my name.*

The present is full of mercenary forgetfulness
By Yolanda Delgado-Batista

Part I. *On the savage frontier*

In March 2021, the writer Jorge Majfud published his latest historical essay book, *The Savage Frontier. 200 Years of Anglo-Saxon Fanaticism in Latin America*. The limited edition by Rebelde Editores aimed for distribution in the U.S. academic world. As this year comes to a close, the legendary Spanish publishing house Baile del Sol is releasing a new edition of this book, which, despite its 700 pages, has already garnered critics and followers, especially in a context of "cultural war" between revisionists like Majfud and reactions from political figures such as Donald Trump and Jair Bolsonaro, who consider it necessary to impose "patriotic education" in schools and universities.

Yolanda D-Batista: Thank you very much, Professor Majfud, for giving us your attention, knowing how busy you are. I'd like to start this conversation by asking you about one of your latest works, The Savage Frontier, praised by intellectuals like Ariel Dorfman, Noam Chomsky and a journalist like Víctor Hugo Morales. A summary and selection of this book was published in English as Borders of The Wild Frontier: US American Mythology on Latin America. I know it's difficult to ask you to summarize a work of more than 650 pages...

Jorge Majfud: There are several ways to summarize this book, like any other. Basically, it covers the last two centuries of aggressions, from the mythological Daniel Boone, to the interventions from Washington (the political power) and U.S. corporations (the economic and narrative power) in what we imprecisely know today as Latin America, including a large part of the United States. From the start, I take the founding myths of the United States, those narratives that surround us every day, and try to explain, in a historical sequence, how narrative and reality are diametrically opposed...

YDB: For example?

JM: Well, for example, the great national fragmentation (into classes, like millionaires and the millions of indebted, all grouped in the same church, into races or ethnicities of slaves and slave owners, of poor ghettos and rich congressmen, into regions, like the North against the South) and, on the other hand, the obsessive idea of Union: one flag, one God, one homeland "in perpetual danger." For example, the Anglo-Saxon mentality's obsession with enslaving and controlling, hidden behind the mask of "the fight for democracy and freedom." The slaveholding expansion of the minority but powerful South was carried out in the name of liberty, of civilization, and of the "blessing of slavery." All this later translated into the idea that it is millionaire entrepreneurs who create jobs and benefit the dangerous workers. The love for guns and the hatred for unions, which were very strong after the Civil War, are a translation or a travesty of the previous slaveholding culture of the master, guarantor of God, of order, and of freedom against the demonized slave who sought to destroy prosperity and morality. The myth that "we are a nation of laws" systematically clashes with the violation of all laws and treaties that ceased to be beneficial for the owners of the guns. The idea that "we bring democracy to Latin America" clashes with hundreds of examples against it and none in favor. But if reality doesn't conform to our desire, too bad for reality. In fact, Washington has been the greatest promoter of communism in Latin America.

YDB: Are we talking about the past?

JM: Yes. About the past and the present, as always when we speak of founding myths. They are more alive than sequoias. Ask any university student why Texas became independent in 1836, and they'll tell you it was to "free the Americans from Mexican tyranny." They don't say it was because the Mexicans gave them land and committed the sin of outlawing slavery. And when the Mexicans realized their mistake, they outlawed immigration from the north, and the white fanatics continued crossing the border illegally. And so we can go on with the Banana Republics, the massacres of Black people as sport down there in the tropics of the world, all to save the "superior race" that had to endure the responsibility of saving civilization. Rudyard Kipling's mythical poem "The White Man's Burden" summed it up perfectly, and U.S. politicians never tired of quoting it. When they discovered they were a minority in Creation, they panicked, as usual, and began a remake of slaveholder rhetoric: they had to avoid "white genocide," the disappearance of the "beautiful race," the "superior race."

YDB: We've heard it recently...

JM: Yes, nothing new. That entire tradition has returned, this time brazenly, without the masks of political correctness. I think in the 19th century, the paranoia worsened when whites finished colonizing the world and discovered they weren't the majority of Creation and their beautiful daughters could fall prey to temptation from big, dark penises or, worse, a Haiti-style revolt. This is in the letters of many racist leaders and politicians of the time... It's no coincidence that wars and imperialism were considered a man's business. And they still are. That sexual obsession that, until not long ago, surfaced when the precandidates Marco Rubio and Donald Trump debated on national television about the size of the penis of the man who would eventually become president. People don't vote for intellectually superior candidates but for those who represent them in some way, whether by color or by the size of their penis. A pornographic imagination that led to thousands of lynchings just in the United States. The lynching law was only abolished last year, and not without resistance. Not so the obsession with guns, which has the same origin and is still in force and will be for centuries to come, as it is the country's second most important religion.

YDB: Recently, books about Latin America with an opposite interpretation have been published... It's said that the vision

of La frontera salvaje seeks to absolve Latin Americans of respon-
sibility for their own problems…

JM: … and that Latin Americans are underdeveloped because they read Eduardo Galeano, right? Pure propaganda,
very old but very much alive thanks to big publishing houses
and media conglomerates. Of course, Latin Americans also
bear responsibility for their problems, but the radical question is: *What social and ideological package are we talking about?*
Reactionaries are experts at assembling political combos,
where they bundle God and the Free Market into the same
menu, like McDonald's bundles hamburgers, fries, and
Coca-Cola, with ten pseudo-toxic variations. You want to eat
a burger and end up addicted to the other two. That is, you
believe in God and end up defending the Merchants that Jesus himself drove out of the temple.

YDB: Latin America and its own responsibility would be one
of those combos.

JM: Exactly, just as it's another combo to talk about "the
United States" when millions of Americans opposed and
continue to oppose imperialist aggression and abuses, more
so than millions of Latin Americans. That's why in *La fron-*
tera salvaje I emphasize "Washington" (as a political power,
as a tool of its wealthy corporations, as the hub of its illegal
secrets) rather than "the United States," which is a continent-
country, full of contradictions and dissenters, thanks to
whom history is not even more tragic than it is.

YDB: So, Latin Americans are also responsible for their real-
ity, but not all equally.

JM: Without a doubt. Because the responsibility of the tortured, the disappeared, the millions massacred (200,000 in Guatemala alone, thanks to the CIA), mostly indigenous, Black, or poor whites, is not the same as the responsibility of the traditional oligarchy in the Southern countries. Dictatorships are also not the consequence of the so-called guerrillas who emerged after a century of genocides, massacres, and social atrocities. But the oligarchy and their lackeys find it convenient to repeat this nonsense, often citing a very limited history. Let's recall the universal logic mentioned by the Peruvian González Prada, the Ecuadorian Juan Montalvo in the 19th century, and the American Malcolm X last century: the Indians, the house negroes were the primary defenders of the oppression of their brothers in the fields.

YDB: The reference to the oligarchy sounds like sixties rhetoric…

JM: Let it sound, and let it sound loudly, like Galileo's *Eppur si muove*. Those, the Latin American oligarchs, are indeed the first responsible for the dictatorships, the massacres, the injustices, the exploitation, the premature deaths, and the misery of millions in our societies. Let them publish a thousand books and millions of newspapers and magazines, let them give a hundred thousand, a million subscribers to the new mercenaries on YouTube, now labeled as "influencers," but no one can change the hard and dark history. To forget this glaring reality, at least while the truth remains dangerous, there are the mercenaries of the pen and the selfie, some salaried, others honorary enthusiasts. These mercenaries, voluntary and involuntary, supported by the millions of the CIA and by the organizations that channel "aid" like USAID, NED and so many other foundations, have spent decades victimizing the victims by accusing them of self-victimization. Even today, books promoted by large publishing conglomerates are still being published, portraying "Latin Americans" as irresponsible people who blame the United States and Europe for their underdevelopment, that the past is and doesn´t matter... They have no sense of decency.

YDB: Do you believe the books are promoted by certain corporate interests? That is, do you believe culture is manipulated by external forces, politically speaking?

JM: Of course. We have an idealized image of culture that comes from old encyclopedias. Time is the best judge, but sometimes it takes one or two centuries to pass judgment. Isn't the Market somewhat external to culture? Let's say the market is part of culture, but not its director. Aren't the millions of dollars, channeled through various foundations, if not directly and secretly, determining factors in the sale and circulation of certain ideas, certain ethical and aesthetic sensibilities? You'd have to be very, very naive to believe the answer is no.

YDB: In The Wild Frontier *there are several stories that reveal these manipulations in culture and the press.*

JM: Yes, in a concrete way and based on declassified documents. In the recent past (and there's no reason to think it's any different now), the CIA, the ideological police of the United States abroad (with occasional incursions into domestic territory, much to the FBI's displeasure), promoted certain books and suppressed those that were inconvenient, often without the authors even knowing. Of course, the CIA's help isn't even necessary, because the powerful interests of the Latin American and North Atlantic oligarchy are more than enough. There are no secrets here: some books are condemned to obscurity, while others are elevated to Olympus, regardless of their literary quality or the relevance of their truths. The same goes for awards.

YDB: According to this thesis, external, imperial interventions were and are decisive in the reality of countries in the Global South, say Latin America, Africa...

JM: Without a doubt. Not just decisive in the countries of the South, but also in the North. Reality isn't made up of Platonic absolutes; any relative difference is decisive. Those who deny it could start by returning the thousands of tons of gold and silver they took, which still contribute to the stability of their wise economies. If the psychological and cultural past of countries doesn't matter in the present (another absurd hypothesis), that tangible and audible past still weighs heavily in the coffers of the rich. Like their beautiful cities, the gold and silver continue to work, even as they sleep in the vaults of major banks. Not to mention the tragedy of Africa. Or did all those metals evaporate like guano in the impoverished soils of Europe?

YDB: But the Anglo-Saxons have always been more pragmatic and focused on the present.

JM: Because they practice forgetfulness as a tradition. It's also never mentioned anywhere that the practice of self-victimization has been consistent on the Anglo-Saxon side: every time the settlers, the slaveholders, or the governments in Washington wanted to take more land and more wealth from their neighbors (Indians, Mexicans, and any people who fell within the Frontier), they invented false attacks and repeated them ad nauseam: "we were attacked first," "we had to defend ourselves," "we will never forget," though forgetfulness has been a central strategy. The same people who violated every national border (borders) would return to their country and arm themselves against poor immigrants, expelled from those same invaded and destroyed countries, repeating, "this is a country of laws, and we must protect our borders"; "there's no racism in wanting to protect the laws." As if the laws themselves weren't racist. It's also never said that imperialism is a massive and radical racism against which there are no outraged marches from the hypersensitive kids of the Snowflake Generation, protectors of politically correct language. A president can kill a hundred Black people in the name of freedom and "our right to defend ourselves" (in foreign countries), but if he says the word "nigger," he loses his job, as several professors have lost theirs for reading racist documents in their classes that included this word. Hypocrisy on steroids. When it's discovered that in the Middle East a drone killed fifty children, no one sheds a tear, because those children don't exist. So let's talk about racism and fanaticism. In fact, there is a continuity of the ideas and values of the slaveholding South with the policies and military actions of the supposedly victorious Union. The Confederates were the only ones who came close to destroying the United States, as they did with Mexico, to continue expanding slavery over "inferior" peoples and races, and today their most radical heirs consider themselves the essence of patriotism and freedom, when in reality they were the root and inspiration for nefarious figures like Adolf Hitler. Something even Hitler himself acknowledged.

YDB: You mention that in the second part of The Wild Frontier…

JM: The book is composed of three parts: *Por tierra, Por mar y Por aire*. In that regard, I'm very old-fashioned: I believe that imperialism existed and still exists. Strategically, this word has been turned into a taboo. But it would be cowardly not to use it. This tragic history would not have been possible, or would have been very different, without the fear, paranoia, and racial and religious fanaticism (like Manifest Destiny) that inspired every conquest, every intervention, every coup d'état, every massacre in the name of freedom and human rights. Something that continues today, but with the predictable embellishments of political and social narratives. I don't claim it to be a perfect book, because that doesn't exist, especially when I wrote it in nine months with frenetic intensity. After that, I spent a year without writing any books. The one with the University of Valencia publishing house, *La privatización de la Verdad* (*The Privatization of the Truth*), also published this year, was mostly written long before. In any case, as you say, it's hard to summarize 650 pages in a single answer, but not impossible. The title is, almost always, the most radical synthesis of any book. It is in this case.

YDB: In addition to your profession as a professor at Jacksonville University, you are a fiction writer. What do you most appreciate and most detest about this craft?

JM: I'm not sure I could define writing as a craft. I don't make a living from writing, nor do I do it out of obligation. For me, literature, both in reading and writing, provides me with two seemingly contradictory feelings: refuge and liberation.

Majfud, about Neofeudalism a decade ago

Here we rescued a dialogue between Gabriel Conte and the writer Jorge Majfud, produced in 2014, in which he anticipated what is now called *techno-feudalism* and which he envisioned as a *Neofeudalism*, now accompanied by the empire of social networks, algorithms, and AI.[4]

---

[4] Gabriel Conte, journalist and writer, author of a dozen books of essays and literature. The original interview was published in *MDZ Mundo*, on March 23, 2014. www.mdzol.com/mundo/2014/3/29/que-democracias-nos-promete-la-nueva-guerra-fria-917537.html and republished 11 years later by the same outlet under the title "Thinker Majfud and a Preview from a Decade Ago on Neofeudalism"

The United States heading toward a tech-dominated Middle Ages

"The worst thing that can happen to a democracy is to leave politics in the hands of politicians". The phrase is provocatively launched from his office at Jacksonville University in the United States by Jorge Majfud, the Uruguayan who is one of the most prominent Latin American-origin writers in that country.

In recent months, there has been a *lull* in the media presence of the author. Precisely when—in any case—he was needed most, so to speak, to decode a reality that the media often strive not to analyze but rather to mirror (often distortedly) other media.

He launches his provocation at a time when popularly elected governments are overthrown prematurely; when some countries openly decide what will happen tomorrow inside another; and when the world order is disrupted by off-schedule geopolitical maneuvers. We take his remark as an opportunity to dive deeper into the present, knowing that the outcome of this conversation will never be the hypnotization of the reader, but rather a kick toward critical thinking.

GABRIEL CONTE: *It's been a while since we've read your columns in the newspapers…*

JORGE MAJFUD: When I found out that 85 people in the world possessed the same wealth as half of the world's population, I realized that everything had been said. Since I never wanted to be rich, I would have been indifferent to this fact if those who are dying to be rich would stop governing us.

GC: *Is that ironic?*

JM: A little. But it's also true.

GC: *How do "the rich" govern us?*

JM: More than the rich, who are almost the new proletariat, it's the ultra-rich, the corporations, which becomes a new paradox, since if money during the Renaissance meant the end of aristocracy and its class and blood privileges, today that same money has created a *Neofeudalism* where corporations are closed duchies and principalities, with some highly publicized exceptions, obviously. Now, if you look at the disproportionality of wealth ownership, you'll realize who has the ability to dictate narratives and who is simply wasting their time replicating them. It's a dialectical exercise, similar to the tournaments held in ancient Greece. Pure dialectical sport. Lately, I've become disenchanted with the possibilities of this type of struggle. I'll probably return, because it's not easy to quit a vice, but I'm no longer the optimistic young man I was decades ago. On the other hand, I'm also a little disenchanted by how the "football mentality" dominates dialectical disputes. Some take one side, others take the other, and everything they read or say serves to defend their ideas rather than question their own.

Though I admire José Martí, I disagree with his optimism that "trenches of ideas are worth more than trenches of stone." Yes, they are worth more, but how much harm they also do.

GC: *Can we still believe in politics?*

JM: That question contains an epistemological assumption older than Amenhotep IV: truth exists and is unique. In politics, there are no truths, there are interests. Of course, we can also measure it from a moral standpoint. Therefore, the answer to that question is yes and no. While politics is a fundamental area of human existence, few things are more superficial than political opinions.

Worse: we can see that there is still a strong intoxication of politics in many countries, like in Venezuela or the United States, which is as deadly as radical indifference.

Now, beyond all relativisms, we can think that there must be a few fixed points, such as tolerance, which is so lacking today in so many parts of the world. If it's not political hatreds, it's religious hatreds or sports hatreds or national hatreds that nowadays reduce themselves to measuring the size of GDP. While a few benefit from so much hatred, the rest practice it: some ideas and passions serve private corporations, others serve the strongmen of the moment. All of them, always, have understandable excuses to stay in power.

GC: *Where are we headed in politics, then?*

JM: In the 1990s, against the neoliberal wave that celebrated the defeat of the weak, I was of the opinion that history was moving from representative democracy to direct democracy. In 2003, it seemed to me that the option was still in motion, although I continued to publish that after a major economic and systemic crisis resulting from the war in Iraq and social movements of disobedience, humanity would be torn between more democracy or more state control. For some obscure reason, I still believe we are heading toward greater direct democracy, but the present seems to contradict my prediction and, on the contrary, shows us a strong advance of non-traditional totalitarianisms.

GC: *Democracy is not just about voting. Every so often, the dictator Stroessner would hold plebiscites to legitimize himself. In North Korea, China, and Cuba, there are "elections," although not multiparty ones. What quality would this "direct democracy" you speak of have? On a very local level? Would it revert to opportunistic dialogue with the masses to validate decisions? What will happen to the political party system?*

JM: Cuba was a Revolution in the 60s, one of the most important of the 20th century. Today it is a conservative regime, clinging to a religion. By direct democracy, I meant the ability of the people to make decisions immediately or, at least, not conditioned by electoral cycles. Representatives no longer represent anything more than a tradition, like the kings of old Europe. They are remnants of historical inertia.

However, the maturity of the Disobedient Society is much further off than I thought twenty years ago. Its main instruments, communication networks, are still not true democratic tools; they are still toys.

I say still, as a faint glimmer of optimism...

GC: *For example?*

JM: ...For example, the financial totalitarianism of Western democracies (or whatever they're called, though I prefer a democracy in quotation marks to a dictatorship in capital letters), for example, the astronomical control of the hyper-government of the United States due to new technologies, completely contrary to its founding values. For example, the less abstract authoritarianism of partisan or personalist governments like those in China and Russia, or the clumsy personalism of Maduro in Venezuela, etc.

GC: *Is the United States headed toward a form of totalitarianism?*

JM: In many ways, it already is, though in others, we still have something called laws that, fortunately, are the last resort of those without power.

Like ancient Athens under Pericles, it is a democracy within its borders and an arrogant power outside them.

Of course, just as the Athenians justified themselves to the complaints of Sparta and other peoples by saying "you complain because you can't do it like we can," any other option would be the same. Or worse, if we consider a China or Russia with the same capacity to create and destroy as the United States. But this last part is pure speculation.

GC: *Has American society become more radical?*

JM: No. At least from a humanistic perspective, society is less fundamentalist than it was in the fifties or even the eighties. Now the true nature of this country, which consists of an overwhelming diversity, is much better accepted. Personally, this is the characteristic that most excites me about this country: its infinite diversity, that fertile obviousness that is so hard to see from the outside. But if we are to judge the popular sentiments derived from its social narratives, perhaps we can abuse an aphorism and say that there are two kinds of people who hate the enormous diversity of the United States: one is the anti-Americans; the others are Americans... those nationalists who in every country pretend to be the true citizens. Now, when I speak of the totalitarianism of the United States, I'm not referring to society, perhaps not even to the current government, but to the mega-corporations and the control systems exercised by government apparatuses: control of individuals, violation of their privacy, control of social narratives, etc. Like all totalitarianisms, it is not total. Less so this paradoxical product of such a diverse and complex country. The mere fact that we can criticize it is an indication that demonstrates this, I think.

GC: *So it's still a country of laws.*

JM: Yes. However, corporations and lobbies manage very well to ensure that laws are not an obstacle, that is, to extend their powers without needing to violate written laws. For example, while the nearly infinite capacity of the NSA, a government agency that surpasses any imaginary Big Brother, may be considered illegal from some perspectives, or at least questionable from a constitutional or moral standpoint, the overwhelming power of corporations in shaping public opinion is perfectly legal. The problem is that the solutions to limit this private power have, at least in the experience of other countries like Venezuela, consisted of the abuse of state power, which has not solved the problem but instead created others. Venezuela, radicalized to its detriment, one party or the other may challenge the traditional families, the owners of major media, in terms of their ability to generate "public opinion" through the not-so-recommendable method of conflict and proscription. On the contrary, governments should foster dissent and individual freedom (the only real freedom) in all its possible forms.

For this, I would insist on something I've repeated for years: the worst thing that can happen to a democracy is to leave politics in the hands of politicians.

A government should welcome criticism and protest, if necessary, and strive to integrate dissenters, who are and always should be part of society.

Perhaps Uruguay is one of those concrete examples of political tolerance on our continent. We can discuss everything, we can question everything, but in a democracy, tolerance is the only possible political truth.

GC: *American intellectuals always talk about "the corporations," but can we be more precise, for example, in how these groups supposedly operate?*

JM: It's very simple: they don't need to own any media. It's enough for them to be the primary advertisers. For example, if I own the largest soap factory in my town and the newspaper and all its employees, journalists, and other workers depend on my advertisements, surely none of them would investigate my business, not even their columnists would insist on attacking my political ideas week after week. That, more or less, is what happens on a large scale in the developed world today. In the past, newspapers were more independent because they relied on sales of their copies, but today that income is minimal, if not symbolic.

GC: *Where is U.S. politics headed?*

JM: I fear the United States is heading toward ethnic politics, at least on a partisan level. From a humanistic and democratic perspective, it makes no sense that one can guess someone's political preferences just by looking at their skin color or their place of residence, but the concrete fact is that this is currently the case. Previously, this predictability came fundamentally from social classes. To some extent, in Latin America, hatreds remain class-based but, above all, they are ideological hatreds, which serve as a substitute for the religious hatreds of Europe's past, which, for its part, has turned to nationalist disputes.

In other words, Latin America has stagnated in the 20th century, Europe has regressed to the Early Modern era of the 18th and 19th centuries, and the United States, as always, is headed toward breaking all barriers and practicing a politics of the Middle Ages and, in a few years, a politics of the caves, where ethnicity is more important than religious and ideological superstitions.

Be that as it may, the antidote to avoid catastrophe lies in the novelty introduced by Renaissance humanists and the Enlightenment of the Early Modern era: tolerance for diversity, even if not the recognition of its constitutional nature.

GC: *What is the model to follow in the world?*

JM: Perhaps there shouldn't be a model. Maybe a historical tendency, maybe a natural condition of the human being, which could be summarized as anarchy. However, although humanity in the last nine hundred years has taken great strides toward this utopia, it remains a utopia and probably will always be so. The balance, therefore, lies in the greatest possible individual freedom and the minimal authority and control by a minority group, be it the state or private corporations, which so resemble the principalities of the Middle Ages and the Renaissance.

GC: *From your perspective, are we heading toward a new bipolarity with a "Cold War" between the U.S. plus Europe against Russia, Chavista America, Iran, and China?*

JM: It already exists; there's been a new Cold War brewing for some time.

To some extent, Russia resembles the humiliated Germany of the interwar period: a former empire in the oldest style of annexing territories, now experiencing a nationalist revival. On the other hand, the Western powers are conducting their usual business, albeit with some risks, as in the case of Europe. For the United States, despite the criticism conservatives level at Obama, the situation is far more favorable than it seems. It provides the perfect excuse to take part in another Eastern European country, torn apart by the interests of opposing powers. As I wrote more than a decade ago, the Arab and Persian countries are merely a distraction in a broader conflict: the United States and Europe on one side, and China and Russia on the other. But I wouldn't call it bipolarity, though the human mind always tends toward bipolar confrontations. I would say multipolar with dominant powers.

GC: *A few days ago, I reviewed the forecasts from think tanks for 2014. The one that got the most press at the end of 2013 didn't say a word about Ukraine, except for what it saw at the time: "an internal crisis." Is the world becoming more unpredictable due to the speed with which strategies collapse and secret data is released thanks to people like Assange or Snowden? Or is it that "everything is out of control"?*

JM: The world is not unpredictable, but its complexity is so overwhelming that no one can foresee everything. That has always been the case. Still, what's happening in Ukraine is not so grave. Everyone is making a great business out of it, except the Ukrainians, which is part of a historical pattern, especially in the region.

When have world powers not taken advantage of interventions in Eastern European countries? It has been happening for centuries and will continue to happen.

www.ingramcontent.com/pod-product-compliance
Lightning Source LLC
Chambersburg PA
CBHW032102280326
41933CB00009B/735